THE TWENTY ECUMENICAL COUNCILS
OF THE CATHOLIC CHURCH

Nihil obstat

        Fr. Benvenutus Ryan, O.F.M.
        Censor Librorum

Nihil Obstat

        Arthur J. Scanlan, S.T.D.
        Censor Librorum

Imprimi potest

        Fr. Mathias Faust, O.F.M.,
        Min. Provincialis

Imprimatur

        Patrick Cardinal Hayes,
        † *Archbishop of New York*

New York, August 8, 1936

THE TWENTY ECUMENICAL COUNCILS
OF THE
CATHOLIC CHURCH

BY
FATHER CLEMENT RAAB, O.F.M.

LORETO PUBLICATIONS
FITZWILLIAM, NEW HAMPSHIRE, USA
A. D. 2012

1937 First Edition Published By
LONGMANS, GREEN AND CO.
114 FIFTH AVENUE, NEW YORK
221 EAST 20TH STREET, CHICAGO
88 TREMONT STREET, BOSTON

LONGMANS, GREEN AND CO. LTD.
39 PATERNOSTER ROW, LONDON, E C 4
6 OLD COURT HOUSE STREET, CALCUTTA
53 NICOL ROAD, BOMBAY
36A MOUNT ROAD, MADRAS

LONGMANS, GREEN AND CO.
215 VICTORIA STREET, TORONTO

2012 Edition Published by
LORETO PUBLICATIONS
P.O. BOX 603 FITZWILLIAM, N.H. 03447
WWW.LORETOPUBS.ORG • 603.239.6671

ALL RIGHTS RESERVED • 2012
ISBN 978-1-930278-73-8

PRINTED IN THE UNITED STATES OF AMERICA

FOREWORD

The Church is essentially conservative. Her conservatism is not merely a measure of prudence and good judgment; it is an intrinsic necessity. No matter what she may consider, decide or undertake, she always harks back to the beginning. Keenly sensitive to every new movement, every stir, every breath in the world about her, she seeks to make her words and actions intelligible and convincing amid new conditions and new demands. And the marvel is that every readjustment bears the earmark of the venerable refrain: "Sicut erat in principio, et nunc, et semper." Pope Stephen's Latin might have offended the ears of classicists, but his uncompromising words carried a classical principle when he bluntly declared "Nihil innovetur nisi quod traditurn est." And in this the Church distinguishes herself from other earthly organizations. The latter, in order to survive, to function and prosper, must look forward and move forward; they must adapt themselves to ever-changing conditions, demands and opportunities. They must either conform or capitulate, whereas the Church by calmly rehearsing the same old truths in clearer accents, commands universal attention. And so, after these twenty centuries the "pillar and ground of truth" has not moved a whit from her primitive position, while all other human foundations have either crumbled to dust or have been driven headlong by the maelstrom of this fast changing world. To these, the ideal looms hazily in the distant future; to the Church, it stands firmly in the distant past. The closer she aligns herself with Christ, the surer she is of ultimate success and victory, being "built upon the foundation of the apostles and prophets, Jesus Christ himself being the chief cornerstone." (Eph. II. 20).

While there is no essential difference between a pronouncement ex cathedra and a dogmatic definition of an ecumenical council, still, no one will gainsay that a great deal more human interest and human authority attaches to the latter. The former proceeds from the Head alone; the latter, from both Head and members, acting in perfect unison. At an ecumenical council the Church arises in all her power and dignity. She is stirred within herself and every fiber senses the solemnity of the hour. The successors of the Apostles have come from every land to testify with the Successor of Peter "quod ubique, quod semper, quod ab omnibus creditum est," as St. Vincent of Lerins puts it. This makes the study of the councils not only an important issue, but affords perhaps more color, variety and sympathetic concern than any other topic in our ecclesiastical curriculum.

If the history of the Church be compared to a river, we might well say that in this long stream the twenty councils stand out as so many waterfalls, where all the currents assemble, where debris and dirt are deposited, where the waters are purified, and where the river gathers new force and speed for its onward journey. And as the wanderer will be naturally impelled to stop near the waterfall, even so will the student of history feel an urge to rivet his attention upon this phenomenon in ecclesiastical life. In fact the ecumenical councils are the chief points of interest to the student of theology and religion. For some decades past down to this day history holds a leading position in all ecclesiastical studies. Every subject in the curriculum is prefaced by a historical survey. As a result, we have the History of Dogma, the History of Liturgy, the History of the Bible, the History of Moral Theology, the History of Ascetical Theology. Meanwhile Church History proper is still imbued with the responsibility over the entire field. This condition has its advantages, but some day the matter will become cumbersome, if not confusing. And if someone should some day succeed in synthesizing all this historical material, he would most likely concentrate upon the councils as the strategic points in the development of the "magisterium, ministerium, imperium" of the living Church. From the councils, the nerve centers in Christ's Mystical Body, every act, every decree and every movement reaches both backward and forward either as a check on some error or abuse or as a stimulus to some point of doctrinal development, or to some wholesome reform, or to some phase of religious life of the Church.

The present volume is designed to serve as a ready survey and reference book on the history of the councils. It does not pretend to enrich the findings of the scholars; nor does it propose to enter upon a discussion of moot questions and problems. It is to serve as an aid primarily to the cleric or lay student who has neither the time nor the opportunity to delve into, and analyze sources and controversies, but who is satisfied to learn the outstanding facts and findings concerning which Church historians generally agree. This brief and positive sketch of the twenty great events in history, so vibrant with life and so far-reaching in their consequences, will afford him, we trust, a very definite and appreciable knowledge of the nature and history of Holy Mother Church.

Father Thomas Plassmann, O.F.M.

St. Bonaventure, New York
Feast of St. Bonaventure
July 14, 1936

AUTHOR'S REMARKS

The separate treatise of the Twenty Ecumenical Councils of the Catholic Church is meant primarily for seminarians, for students of Church History and for study clubs. Some may find it strange that there is an absence of footnotes. The reasons for this omission are that, as a rule, seminarians have no time to read the various quotations and they do not have at their disposal the books from which the quotations are taken. Others who are anxious to make a more comprehensive study of the Councils will find ample material by consulting the authors mentioned in the Bibliography.

Father Clement Raab, O.F.M.

St. Francis Monastery, New York City

SYNOPSIS OF THE
TWENTY ECUMENICAL COUNCILS
OF THE CATHOLIC CHURCH

FIRST ECUMENICAL COUNCIL   Page 1
Place: Nicaea
Time: 325
Pope: St. Sylvester I, 314–335
Emperor: Constantine the Great, 306–337
Work of the Council: Condemnation of the heresy of Arius by clearly defining the consubstantiality of God the Son with God the Father.

SECOND ECUMENICAL COUNCIL   Page 5
Place: Constantinople (first).
Time: 381
Pope: St. Damascus I, 367–384
Emperor: Theodosius the Great, 379–394
Work of the Council: Condemnation of the heresy of Macedonius by clearly defining the divinity of the Holy Ghost.

THIRD ECUMENICAL COUNCIL   Page 8
Place: Ephesus
Time: 431
Pope: St. Celestine I, 423–432
Emperor: Theodosius II, 408–450
Work of the Council: Condemnation of the heresy of Nestorius by clearly defining the divine maternity of the Blessed Virgin Mary.

FOURTH ECUMENICAL COUNCIL   Page 13
Place: Chalcedon.
Time: 451
Pope: St. Leo I, the Great, 440–461
Emperor: Marcian, 450–457
Work of the Council: Condemnation of the heresy of Eutyches.

Fifth Ecumenical Council   Page 19
Place: Constantinople (second).
Time: 553
Pope: Vigilius, 540–555
Emperor: Justinian I, 527–565
Work of the Council: Condemnation of the "Three Chapters."

Sixth Ecumenical Council   Page 23
Place: Constantinople (third).
Time: 680
Pope: St. Agatho, 678–682
Emperor: Constantine IV, 668–685
Work of the Council: Condemnation of the heresy of the Monothelites.

Seventh Ecumenical Council   Page 29
Place: Nicaea (second).
Time: 787
Pope: Hadrian I, 772–795
Emperor: Constantine VI, 780–801
Work of the Council: Condemnation of iconoclasm.

Eighth Ecumenical Council   Page 33
Place: Constantinople (fourth).
Time: 869
Pope: Hadrian II, 867–872
Emperor: Basil, 867–896
Work of the Council: Removal of the schism caused by Photius.

Ninth Ecumenical Council   Page 37
Place: Lateran in Rome (first).
Time: 1123
Pope: Callistus II, 1118–1124
Emperor: Henry V, 1106–1125
Work of the Council: Confirmation of the Concordat of Worms and abolition of the strife over investiture.

Tenth Ecumenical Council Page 41
Place: Lateran in Rome (second).
Time: 1139
Pope: Innocent II, 1130–1143
Emperor: Conrad III, 1137–1152
Work of the Council: Abolition of the papal schism and condemnation of the heresy of Peter of Bruys.

Eleventh Ecumenical Council Page 44
Place: Lateran in Rome (third).
Time: 1179
Pope: Alexander III, 1159–1181
Emperor: Frederick Barbarossa, 1152–1190
Work of the Council: Regulation of election of a pope and condemnation of the Albigensian heresy.

Twelfth Ecumenical Council Page 47
Place: Lateran in Rome (fourth).
Time: 1215
Pope: Innocent III, 1198–1216
Emperor: Otto IV, 1208–1215
Work of the Council: Recovery of the Holy Land, reform of discipline, condemnation of the Albigensian heresy.

Thirteenth Ecumenical Council Page 52
Place: Lyons in France (first).
Time: 1245
Pope: Innocent IV, 1241–1254
Emperor: Frederick II, 1215–1250
Work of the Council: The excommunication of Frederick II.

Fourteenth Ecumenical Council Page 55
Place: Lyons in France (second).
Time: 1274
Pope: St Gregory X, 1271–1276
Emperor: Rudolph of Habsburg, 1273–1291
Work of the Council: Help for the Holy Land, union of the Greeks with the Latins, reform of morals.

FIFTEENTH ECUMENICAL COUNCIL   Page 60
Place: Vienne in France.
Time: 1311–1314
Pope: Clement V, 1305
Emperor: Henry VII, 1308–1313
Work of the Council: (1) The case of the Knights Templars; (2) help for the Holy Land; (3) reform of morals.

SIXTEENTH ECUMENICAL COUNCIL   Page 65
Place: Constance.
Time: 1414
Pope: Gregory XII, 1406–1417
            Martin V, 1417–1431
Emperor: Sigismund, 1410–1437
Work of the Council: (1) Removal of the papal schism; (2) extirpation of heresy; (3) general reformation of the Church in "Head and members."

SEVENTEENTH ECUMENICAL COUNCIL   Page 73
Place: Basel 1431–1437
            Ferrara 1438
            Florence 1439–1443
Time: 1431–1443
Pope: Eugene IV, 1431–1447
Emperor: Albrecht II, 1438–1439
            Frederick III, 1440–1493
Work of the Council: (1) Extirpation of heresy and the Greek schism; (2) re-establishment of peace among Christian Princes; (3) reform of the Church in "Head and members."

EIGHTEENTH ECUMENICAL COUNCIL   Page 84
Place: Lateran in Rome (fifth).
Time: 1512–1517
Pope: Julius II, 1503–1513
            Leo X, 1513–1521
Emperor: Maximilian I, 1493–1519
Work of the Council: (1) The rooting out of schism; (2) the reform of the Church; (3) the crusade against the Turks.

NINTEENTH ECUMENICAL COUNCIL   Page 91
Place: Trent.
Time: 1545–1549 (First Period)
           1551–1552 (Second Period)
           1562–1563 (Third Period)
Pope: Paul III, 1534–1549
           Julius III, 1550–1555
           Plus IV, 1559–1565
Emperor: Charles V, 1519–1556
           Ferdinand I, 1556–1564
Work of the Council: Extirpation of heresy (against the innovators of the 16th century) and reform of morals.

TWENTIETH ECUMENICAL COUNCIL   Page 108
Place: Vatican, Rome.
Time: 1869–1870
Pope: Plus IX, 1864–1878
Work of the Council: Condemnation of existing errors and definition of papal infallibility.

BIBLIOGRAPHY   Page 115
INDEX   Page 116

I
THE FIRST ECUMENICAL COUNCIL
HELD AT NICEA IN 325

WORK OF THE COUNCIL: Condemnation of the heresy of Arius by clearly defining the consubstantiality of God the Son with God the Father.

Among the many wonderful manifestations of religious activity in the Church, the councils or synods hold an important place. In the language of the Church a council is an assembly of ecclesiastics, properly convoked, to consider and to define doctrine or discipline, or other ecclesiastical matters. In this sense we find the word "council" used in the writings of Tertullian, about the year 200 a.d. According to the intention for which these assemblies were convoked and the number of members in attendance, they were divided, on the one hand, into ecumenical councils, and, on the other hand, into general national provincial and diocesan synods. An ecumenical council did not require the presence of all bishops; it sufficed that all bishops or representatives of all ecclesiastical provinces should be invited, and at a considerable number of them from the different Christian countries should actually be present. The council was convoked either by the Pope or by the Emperor, with the consent of the Pope, who presided over it through his legates. The decrees of an ecumenical council had no legal force until the papal confirmation been granted to them.

It is beyond doubt that the origin of councils dates from that of the Apostles, held in Jerusalem about 52 a.d., at which Saints Peter, James, John, Barnabas, and Paul were present. Theologians disagree as to the nature of the councils, whether they are of divine or human authority. The best answer seems to be that they are an apostolic institution, but that the Apostles acted undoubtedly on the instruction of their divine Master; otherwise they could not have published the decrees of this first council with the words: "It hath seemed good to the Holy Ghost and to us...(Acts, xv, 28). The decrees of the first council were four: The converted Gentiles should abstain from things sacrificed to idols from blood; from things strangled; and from fornication (Acts, xv, 29).

In the two hundred and fifty years which followed the Apostolical Council, we read that many synods were held, mostly in Asia Minor, Africa, and Spain: to combat Gnosticism, the negation of positive Christianity; to oppose the heresies of Montanus and Novatianus; to settle the controversy on the celebration of Easter; to define the validity of baptism conferred by heretics; to reclaim to the true Church the Donatists and other heretics.

In the first quarter of the fourth century a new and most formidable heresy arose. It made the convocation of an ecumenical council imperative. The heresy was Arianism, the condemnation of which occasioned the First Ecumenical Council.

Author of Arianism

Arius (250–336), most likely a native of Libya, or as others say, of Alexandria, was a vain and eccentric man. He first espoused the cause of the Meletians, when Meletius, Bishop of Lycopolis, a city in upper Egypt, refused to submit to deposition by his ecclesiastical superior, St. Peter of Alexandria. Abandoning the espousal of this schism, Arius received deaconship at the hands of the latter prelate. But when St. Peter excommunicated the Meletians, the young deacon soon became involved in the same condemnatory sentence. After the martyrdom of St. Peter, his successor, Achillas, restored Arius to communion with the Church, and raised him to the priesthood in 312. He was appointed pastor of a suburban church, called Baucalis. When, in 318, Bishop Alexander, the successor of Achillas, expounded the orthodox doctrine of the Blessed Trinity at a conference of his priests, Arius openly contradicted him, and there promulgated his heretical views. His errors are contained in the following propositions: (1) There was a moment when God was not Father; (2) the Son of God was created from nothing; (3) the Son of God is a creature, and, therefore, He is not eternal; (4) being a creature, the Son of God is subject to change; (5) being a creature, the Son of God is not co-equal with the Father in essence, and only in a figurative sense may we apply to Him the names "God" and "Wisdom of God."

These errors of Arius were condemned by the Synod of Alexandria in 320, at which nearly 100 bishops were present, and by which Arius with all his adherents was excommunicated. In spite of this ecclesiastical censure, Arius continued to exercise his priestly functions. He won over to his side in the controversy Bishop Eusebius of Nicomedia, a distant relative of Emperor Constantine. Arius, exiled by his bishop, went first to Palestine. From there he went to his friend and protector Eusebius of Nicomedia. During his stay at Nicomedia, Arius composed his principal work *Thaleia* ("Banquet"), of which only fragments are still extant in the writings of St. Athanasius. It was written partly in prose and partly in poetry, and contained all the heretical views of Arius. Among his followers, this book had the authority of the Bible.

When unrest and quarrel spread, Emperor Constantine (275–337) intervened. Not understanding the real point at issue in the controversy he wished that Bishop Alexander and Arius should come to an understanding. To effect this reunion and reconciliation, the Emperor sent Bishop Hosius to Alexandria in 324. When this attempt at intervention proved to be a failure, Constantine, at the suggestion of Bishop Hosius, decided to call an ecumenical council.

Proceedings of the Council

Opening of the Council. Constantine addressed most respectful letters to all the bishops, inviting them to a general council, which was to be held at Nicaea in Bithynia in 325. According to the Acts of the Sixth Ecumenical Council, the Emperor convoked this Council of Nicaea in agreement with and by the consent of Pope St. Sylvester (314–335), who appointed as his personal representatives Bishop Hosius and the two Roman priests, Vitus and Vincentius. According to the best authorities, 318 bishops with many priests and deacons (among whom St. Athanasius was the most renowned) came to the council, which opened on May 20 and closed on August 25, 325. The Emperor defrayed all the personal expenses contracted by the bishops in their journey to and stay at the council. The Emperor himself arrived on June 14, 325, and was present at all the sessions of the council until its close. Arius, also, was called to the council. Many bishops of this council were confessors who still bore on their bodies traces of torture and suffering which they had endured for the sake of their faith. There was Paphnutius of Upper Thebais who had undergone fearful tortures in the reign of Maximian and had lost one eye; Potamon of Heraclea who had suffered all but death under Licinius. Others were known for their gifts of prophecy and working miracles, such as James of Nisibis, Spiridion of Cyprus, Nicholas of Myra, Leontius of Caesarea. Still others were renowned for their learning, as Alexander of Alexandria, Eusthatius of Antioch, Marcarius of Jerusalem, and Marcellus of Ancyra.

The work of the council was threefold: (1) the condemnation of the heresy of Arius; (2) the decision on the question of the celebration of Easter; (3) the abolition of the schism of Meletius.

(1) *The condemnation of the heresy of Arius.* The fathers of the council stated the Catholic doctrine against the heresy of Arius in precise terms, declaring that Jesus Christ is really and truly the Son of God, God from all eternity, and that the Son of God is *"Consubstantial"* with the Father. The council drew up a formula of Faith, containing the exact teaching of the Church:

Πιστεύομεν εἰς ἕνα Θεὸν πατέρα παντωκράτερα, ποιητὴν οὐρανοῦ καὶ γῆς, ὁρατῶν τε πάντων καὶ ἀοράτων· καὶ εἰς ἕνα κύριον Ἰησοῦν Χριστὸν τὸν υἱὸν τοῦ Θεοῦ, τὸν μονογενῆ, τὸν ἐκ τοῦ πατρὸς γεννηθέντα πρὸ πάντων τῶν αἰώνων τὸν Θεὸν ἀληθινὸν ἐκ Θεοῦ ἀληθινοῦ, γεννηθέντα, οὐ ποιηθέντα, ὁμοούσιον τῷ πατρί.

Τοὺς δὲ λέγοντας· ἦν ποτε ὅτε οὐκ ἦν, καὶ πρὶν γεννηθῆναι οὐ ἦν καὶ ὅτι ἐκ οὐκ ὄντων ἐγένετο, ἢ ἐξ ἑτέρας ὑποστάσεως ἢ οὐσίας ψάσκοντας εἶναι ἢ τρεπτὸν ἢ ἀλλοιωτὸν τὸν υἱὸν τοῦ Θεοῦ, τούτους ἀναθεματίζει ἡ καθολικὴ καὶ ἀποστολικὴ ἐκκλησία.

"We believe in one God, Father Almighty, Creator of heaven and earth, maker of all things, visible and invisible; and in one Lord Jesus Christ, the Son of God, the only-begotten, born of the Father before all ages, true God of the true God, born, not made, *Consubstantial with the Father.*"

"And those who say there was a time when he was not, and he was not before he was born, and that he was made out of nothing, or of a different substance or essence, saying that the Son of God was changeable and mutable, these the Catholic and Apostolic Church anathematizes."

The formula of faith drawn up by the council is known as the *Nicene Creed*, and is recited during Holy Mass. The word *Consubstantial* became the touchstone of orthodoxy.

All the bishops, except five Arians, signed the profession of faith, and joined in the anathemas which the council pronounced against Arius and his heresy. These five bishops were: Eusebius of Nicomedia, Theognis of Nicaea, Maris of Chalcedon, Theonas of Marmarica, and Secundus of Ptolemais. The Emperor employed his temporal authority to enforce the decisions of the council; he banished Arius to Illyrium. The same fate overtook Theonas and Secundus, the Arians, who remained obstinate to the end. The writings of Arius were ordered to be burnt while those who possessed any of the writings of Arius were commanded to surrender them under penalty of death.

(2) *The decision on the question of the celebration of Easter.* Up to the time of the Council of Nicaea there was a great variety regarding the time of the celebration of Easter. The council forbade the celebration of Easter on the same day with the Jews. It commanded that Easter must be celebrated on the first Sunday which follows the spring full moon. It was ordained that the calculations for the celebration of Easter should be made yearly by the Bishop of Alexandria, who should forward these calculations to the Pope for general publication.

(3) *The abolition of the schism of Meletius.* Bishop Meletius had conferred orders outside of his diocese against the law of the Church. These ordinations were ratified by the council, but Meletius and those ordained by him had to comply with certain conditions.

The council issued also twenty disciplinary canons.

The decrees and canons of the council were signed by Hosius, who had presided at the council, by the two apostolic legates, by the bishops of the council, and by Emperor Constantine, who promulgated in three imperial edicts the decrees of the council as laws of the empire. The Acts of the council were confirmed by Pope St. Sylvester I.

The high esteem in which the Christians of the Orient held the Council of Nicaea may be gathered from the fact that the Greeks, the Syrians, and the Egyptians celebrated an annual feast in honor of the fathers of the council: the Greeks on the Sunday before Pentecost, the Syrians in July, and the Egyptians in November.

II
THE SECOND ECUMENICAL COUNCIL
HELD AT CONSTANTINOPLE IN 381

WORK OF THE COUNCIL: Condemnation of the heresy of Macedonius by clearly defining the divinity of the Holy Ghost.

The Ecumenical Council of Nicaea held in the year 325 dealt the death blow to the heresy of Arius. Protected, however, by the secular power, his heresy lived on. After his miserable death, in which the judgment of God against him was apparent, his followers began to teach other doctrines than those which he had taught them. They became divided into several sects, some of which taught one doctrine, some another. Thus from the great heresy of Arianism arose several others. The principal one of these branch heresies was Macedonianism, named after Macedonius, a semi-Arian Bishop of Constantinople (342), who was a fierce persecutor of the adherents of the faith of Nicaea. He not only expelled those who refused to hold communion with him, but he imprisoned some and brought others before the secular tribunals. On account of his cruelty he was deposed in the year 360, and died about 364.

As Arius had attacked the Second Person of the Blessed Trinity by teaching that the Son of God was not equal to God the Father, so Macedonius attacked the Holy Ghost, the Third Divine Person. He was supported by Marathonius, who was first a government of-ficial, then became a monk and a deacon, and finally Bishop of Nicomedia. (Hence the name of this heresy Macedonianism or Marathonianism). The originators of this heresy held a synod at Zele in Pontus. They separated themselves from the orthodox Church as well as from the Arian Church. They declared that the Holy Ghost was inferior to the Father and to the Son; they called the Holy Ghost a creature of the Son of God.

St. Athanasius (296–373), from whose eagle eye nothing escaped, wrote a treatise in refutation of this new heresy. The orthodox faith was defended in like manner by St. Basil in his work *On the Holy Ghost*, by St. Gregory of Nazianzen in his fifth *Theological Oration*, by Didymus of Alexandria in his books *On the Trinity* and *On the Holy Ghost* and by St. Ambrose of Milan.

A Roman synod held in the year 369, under Pope St. Damasus (366–384), declared that the Father and the Son are of the one divine substance, together with the Holy Ghost. In another Roman synod held in 374 the Pope rejected the teachings of Macedonius as heretical.

In 379 Emperor Gratian had appointed Theodosius his co-emperor to rule over the East. Soon after his baptism, Theodosius issued an edict in which he said "It is our will that all our subjects should follow the religion taught by the Prince of the Apostles to the Romans, and observed by the reigning Pope Damasus, that in conformity with the Gospels and apostolic teaching, we may believe one, only, indivisible Godhead of the Father, the Son and the Holy Ghost. We decree that those alone who thus believe be called Catholics, and that those whose rash and insane impiety we condemn, be called heretics, and that their places of meeting be not called churches."

Theodosius, however, knew well that something more than an expression of the imperial will was needed to pacify the Church in the East, and to suppress its prevalent heresy. He resolved to convoke a council, and selected Constantinople as the place of meeting. He made provision for defraying the expenses of the bishops whom he had summoned. They came from all parts of the East, about 150, besides the 36 bishops who favored the Macedonian heresy, who had also been invited to attend the council. When the bishops were presented to the Emperor, he besought them to restore peace to the Church. He promised to give legal sanction to their decrees, so that the decrees binding in conscience, should be enforced also by the civil power.

Proceedings of the Council

Opening of the Council. The council was opened with due solemnity in the month of May 381, under the presidency of Meletius, Bishop of Antioch. Attempts were made to win back the Macedonians; Theodosius, also, exhorted them to return to the faith and communion of the Church; but they refused and withdrew from the council.

The work of the council was threefold: (1) To provide for the orthodox succession in the episcopal See of Constantinople; (2) to confirm the Nicene Creed by explicit teaching on the Third Person of the Blessed Trinity; (3) to put an end to the Macedonian heresy.

(1) *To provide for the orthodox succession in the episcopal See of Constantinople.* The first measure of the council was to reject Maximus who had usurped the See of Constantinople, and to confirm St. Gregory of Nazianzen as Bishop of Constantinople, who, however, accepted the burden reluctantly. On the death of Meletius, Gregory became president of the council, but on account of differences which arose concerning the successor of Meletius, Gregory resigned the presidency and the bishopric of Constantinople. Nectarius, although he was still a catechumen, was nevertheless chosen Bishop of Constantinople and president of the council.

(2) *To confirm the Nicene Faith by explicit teaching on the Third Person of the Blessed Trinity.* The council drew up a formal treatise on the Catholic doctrine of the Blessed Trinity and a Creed (Nicene-Constantinopolitan Creed). This is an enlargement of the Nicene Creed with emphasis given to the divinity of the Holy Ghost. The Nicene Creed said concerning the Incarnation of the Son of God: "And was incarnate, was made man, suffered, etc." The Creed of Constantinople added: "Was incarnate by the Holy Ghost of the Virgin Mary, and was made man; he was crucified, etc." In regard to the Third Person of the Blessed Trinity, the Creed of Nicaea simply said: "We believe in the Holy Ghost." The Creed of Constantinople unfolded the truth thus:

Πιστεύομεν εἰς τὸ πνεῦμα τὸ ἅγιον, τὸ κύριον καὶ ζωοποιόν, τὸ ἐκ τοῦ πατρὸς ἐκπορευόμενον, τὸ σὺν πατρὶ καὶ υἱῷ προσκυνούμενον καὶ συνδοξαζόμενον, τὸ λαλῆσαν διὰ τῶν προφητῶν.

"We believe in the Holy Ghost, the Lord and Life-giver, who proceeds from the Father, who together with the Father and the Son, is adored and glorified, who spoke through the Prophets."

Thus the divinity of the Holy Ghost was pronounced in clear and precise terms.

(3) *To put an end to the Macedonian heresy.* The council issued four important canons. The first is a dogmatic condemnation of all kinds of Arianism and Macedonianism. The second canon renews the injunctions of the fifth and sixth canon of the Council of Nicaea. (The fifth canon was directed against those who boasted of having obtained church preferment or ordination by money. The sixth canon ordained that provincial synods should be held annually.) The third canon gives to the Bishop of Constantinople a preeminence of honor, because Constantinople is now the new-Rome. The fourth canon declares the ordination of Maximus as Bishop of Constantinople invalid.

Emperor Theodosius received the decrees of the council as oracles of God, and gave them legal force in an imperial decree which he issued on July 30, 381, declaring that the churches should be restored to those bishops who confessed the equal divinity of the Father, the Son, and the Holy Ghost, and who hold communion with Nectarius of Constantinople, Timothy of Alexandria, Pelagius of Laodicea, Amphilochus of Iconium, Gregory of Nyssa, and others, expressly mentioned. Those who hold no communion with the bishops mentioned in the imperial decree, must be expelled from the churches as open heretics.

It is to be noted that this council was composed exclusively of Eastern bishops; neither had it been convoked by the Pope, nor was it presided over by his legates; but it is now reckoned among the ecumenical councils of the Church. The ecumenical character of this council dates among the Greeks from the Council of Chalcedon, held in the year 451, which accepted and solemnly read the Creed of Constantinople with that of Nicaea. In the West, Pope Gregory the Great, following the example of Pope Vigilius and Pope Pelagius II, recognized it as an ecumenical council, but *only in its dogmatical utterances,* by which the true doctrine on the divinity of the Holy Ghost was defined, and heresies denying this article were condemned.

III
THE THIRD ECUMENICAL COUNCIL
HELD AT EPHESUS IN 431

WORK OF THE COUNCIL: Condemnation of the heresy of Nestorius by clearly defining the divine maternity of the Blessed Virgin Mary.

"This is the true faith to believe and confess that our Lord Jesus Christ, the Son of God, is God and man. Although at the same time God and man, there are not in Him two, but only one Christ. One absolutely, not by any confusion of substance, but by unity of person." These words of the renowned Athanasian Creed are the pure expression of apostolic teaching on the great mystery of the Incarnation. Christ is God and Man, yet he is one and the same Person. Thus the Creed has dispelled all the fallacies with which heresy and unbelief have tried to obscure the unchangeable teaching of the Church. The Cerinthians taught that Jesus was a mere man upon whom the Holy Ghost descended in the form of a dove, when he was baptized in the Jordan; but that the same Holy Spirit left Him at the time of His Passion. The Arians, the first radicals of infidelity, were still bolder by denying absolutely the divinity of Jesus Christ. But all the errors concerning the Incarnation may be summed up in general by the heresies of Nestorius and Eutyches. In the present treatise we deal with the heresy of Nestorius and its condemnation by the Third Ecumenical Council which was held at Ephesus in the year 431.

Author of the Heresy

Nestorius, born in Germanicia in Syria, was educated in the school of Theodore of Mopsuestia, priest and monk of Antioch. There he gained some renown as preacher. In 428 he was called by Emperor Theodosius II to the episcopal See of Constantinople. At once he commenced a bitter fight against the Arians. In the beginning of his episcopate, he addressed the Emperor with these words: "Give me the earth, O Emperor, purged of heretics, and I will give heaven to thee; aid me in the destruction of heretics, and I will aid thee in destroying the Persians." Agitated by a tempestuous character, and driven by an ardent desire for fame rather than by a true zeal for faith, Nestorius, in the first year of his episcopate, advanced his heretical views concerning the divinity of Christ and the dignity of the Blessed Virgin Mary, the Mother of God.

He contended that Christ was a mere man, but that he was united with God; that Jesus of Nazareth and the Word of God are two distinct persons; that the Incarnation was simply an indwelling of the Word of God in the man Jesus, as God abides in a temple, so that God was not born, did not suffer and die. From this primary error followed the second, that the Blessed Virgin Mary was not the Θεοτόκος viz. "Mother of God" but only the Χριστοτόκος viz. "Mother of

Christ." Implying that if Mary were the Mother of God, then the Word of God would have a beginning.

As St. Athanasius had been raised up by God to confound the Arians, so St. Cyril of Alexandria was chosen by God to combat the heresy of Nestorius. The latter published his treatise and several homilies on the Incarnation, which he took care to send into Egypt in order to ascertain the views of others. Owing to these writings St. Cyril issued his Easter encyclical to the monks of Egypt, in which he defended the title and dignity of the "Mother of God." Cyril's writings were eagerly read in Constantinople to the great discomfiture and chagrin of Nestorius who had won high favor at the imperial Court. Cyril, in his clear exposition of the Incarnation, informed the Emperor and the imperial family of the new heresy. "Obliged by the old custom of the Church" Cyril reported the heretical teachings of Nestorius to Pope St. Celestine I. Nestorius, also, had written to the Pope, putting the blame of the whole controversy on Cyril, and he recommended in his letter to the Pope that the term "Mother of Christ" should be the golden mean between "Mother of God" and "Mother of man." He also suggested that the Church hold a council, saying that he had already advised the Emperor to this effect.

When Pope Celestine had read the letters of Cyril and Nestorius, he held a synod at Rome in August 430, which decreed that a sentence of excommunication and deposition was to be pronounced against Nestorius, unless he would renounce his errors in an open and written confession within ten days. Pope Celestine, thereupon, addressed epistles to St. Cyril of Alexandria, to Patriarch John of Antioch, to the clergy and laity of Constantinople, and to Nestorius, to acquaint all of them with the decision of the Roman Synod. Cyril, the champion of orthodoxy, was appointed by the Pope to carry out the sentence pronounced by the Roman Synod, should Nestorius persevere in his error.

In the month of November 430, Cyril held a synod of all the bishops of Egypt. The object of this synod was to state in clear terms the doctrine of the Incarnation and divine maternity. A letter, composed by Cyril and endorsed by the synod, was borne to Nestorius by the Bishops Theopantus and Daniel, and two priests of Alexandria, Potamon and Macarius. These messengers handed the document to Nestorius on a Sunday, when he was officiating in his cathedral. In this letter Nestorius was officially informed of the sentence which the Pope had pronounced against him; moreover, he was ordered to reject publicly, in writing, his heretical views; he was furnished with a profession of faith and with twelve anathemas, written by St. Cyril, to which he was ordered to subscribe. Instead of obeying he at once issued twelve counter anathemas, each one of which was a blasphemous contradiction to the corresponding anathemas of Cyril.

On November 19, 430, shortly before Cyril's letter and anathemas had arrived in Constantinople, Emperor Theodosius II had issued an imperial decree, addressed to all metropolitans and bishops, ordering them to convene at Ephesus on Pentecost 431, for the purpose of holding a council. A special invitation to come to the council was extended to St. Augustine, but the messengers returned with the news of St. Augustine's death which had occurred on August 22, 430.

According to the imperial edict the council should open on June 7 (Pentecost), 431. Nestorius, accompanied by sixteen bishops, was the first to arrive in Ephesus; four or five days before Pentecost, Cyril arrived from Alexandria with fifty bishops; a few days after Pentecost they were followed by the Patriarchs Juvenal of Jerusalem and Flavian of Thessalonica with their suffragans; Archbishop Memnon of Ephesus was surrounded by forty suffragan bishops and twelve bishops from Pamphilia. Patriarch John of Antioch had sent word that he would arrive with his suffragans in five or six days. When the Fathers of the council had waited sixteen days after the stipulated time, and John had not yet arrived, Cyril decided to open the council.

Proceedings of the Council

Opening of the Council. The council was formally opened on June 22, 431, in the church dedicated to Mary, the Mother of God. Cyril presided at this session in the name and with the authority of Pope Celestine I.

First Session (June 22, 431). In this session the Nicene Creed, the second epistle of Cyril to Nestorius, the epistle of Pope Celestine to Cyril, and the synodical letter of Alexandria to Nestorius were read. Then, the letter of Nestorius to Cyril was read, and other writings of Nestorius were examined. His teachings were found to be manifestly heretical. Thereupon the council pronounced the sentence of excommunication and deposition against Nestorius, "compelled by the sacred Canons, and by the Epistle of the Most Holy Father Celestine, Bishop of Rome." This sentence of condemnation was signed by 198 bishops, and a number of other bishops added their signature to the document later.

The first session of the council had lasted from morning till night. The inhabitants of Ephesus had waited all day for the decision of the council. When the decision was finally announced that *"Mary is truly the Mother of God,"* the joy of the people knew no bounds. Great was their jubilation, and the bishops were escorted to their houses with torchlights and censers.

On the following day, Nestorius, who had stubbornly rejected three special invitations to attend the first session, was officially notified of his excommunication and deposition by the council.

On June 26 or 27, John of Antioch arrived at Ephesus and was informed of the proceedings of the council. Being a secret friend of Nestorius, he hastily convoked a meeting in his house. Surrounded by 42 bishops, he excommunicated Cyril and Memnon. John with his adherents kept up agitation and spite-work against the proceedings of the council to the very end.

Second Session (July 10, 431). This session was held in the episcopal residence of Memnon. This session was occasioned by the arrival of the papal legates, the Bishops Arcadius and Projectus, and the priest Philip. The epistle of Pope Celestine, addressed to the council, condemning the heresy of Nestorius, was read.

The Fathers acclaimed Celestine as "the new Paul," "the Guardian of Faith." The papal legates, then, demanded an inspection of the acts of the first session.

Third Session (July 11, 431). Again the session took place in the episcopal residence of Memnon. The acts of the first session and all that had been done in reference to the heretic Nestorius, were read once more, and confirmed by the three papal legates.

An official report of all proceedings was sent to the Emperor, with the additional statement that the excommunication and deposition of Nestorius had been approved and confirmed by the papal legates.

Fourth Session (July 16, 431). Held in the church dedicated to the Mother of God. Three bishops were sent to John of Antioch to officially cite him before the council. The bishops returned and reported that they had been disrespectfully repelled by the guards of John. The council declared the sentence of excommunication pronounced by John against Cyril and Memnon null and void.

Fifth Session (July 17, 431). John of Antioch, though cited three times to appear, persisted in his obstinacy. The council, therefore, pronounced the sentence of excommunication against him.

Sixth Session (July 22, 431). Held in the episcopal residence of Memnon. The council ordained that no Creed but the Nicene Creed may be used as the official profession of faith for the Church.

Seventh Session (July 31, 431). Held in the Church of the Mother of God. In this session six disciplinary canons were issued by the council.

Because the imperial mind of Theodosius was perplexed by the conflicting reports of the Ephesine Council on the one hand, and of the pseudo-synod of John of Antioch and his adherents on the other, the fathers of the council thought best to send ambassadors to the court of the Emperor who would explain the true state of affairs. But three days before these messengers of the council arrived at Constantinople, the Count Irenaeus, a friend of Nestorius and John, had already come from Ephesus to the Emperor. When the messengers of the council presented themselves to Emperor Theodosius, they found his mind prejudiced against their cause. The Emperor ordered his almoner, Count John, to go to Ephesus, to depose Cyril, Memnon, and Nestorius, the parties of the dispute, and to settle matters peacefully. Count John's first act was to arrest the three bishops. Horrified by this action, the fathers of the council chose a faithful messenger to carry their letter concealed in the hollow of a reed to the Emperor. In this epistle the bishops refused firmly to communicate with John of Antioch and his followers, unless they would consent to the condemnation of Nestorius; they demanded also the liberation of Cyril and Memnon. In the hollow of the reed they enclosed also a letter addressed to all the bishops, who were then in the capital, and to the clergy of Constantinople. As Theodosius was so beset with supplications, the consequence of this letter was to decide him to receive a delegation of eight from each side. He met the delegates at Chalcedon. After he had heard their respective arguments, he became convinced of the righteousness of the acts of Cyril. The hopes of John of Antioch and his followers were crushed.

On October 25, 431, Maximian was consecrated Bishop of Constantinople to replace the heretic Nestorius, who was banished first to his monastery in Antioch, then later to Egypt, where he ended his life most miserably about 440.

The bishops were now allowed to depart from Ephesus. Cyril, the star of this council, arrived home in Alexandria on October 30, 431, amidst the greatest rejoicings of the people. Pope Celestine confirmed the consecration of Maximian as Bishop of Constantinople on March 15, 432, and bestowed the highest praise upon the Council of Ephesus.

IV
FOURTH ECUMENICAL COUNCIL
HELD AT CHALCEDON IN 451

WORK OF THE COUNCIL: Condemnation of the heresy of Eutyches.

Out of the heresy of Nestorius was evolved another error, equally opposed to the Catholic doctrine of the Incarnation. Not all the opponents of the heretic Nestorius possessed the firm grasp of the truth and the clear perception of St. Cyril of Alexandria. Eutyches (meaning the "fortunate," although some say his name should have been "Atyches," meaning the "unfortunate"), superior of the largest monastery in the vicinity of Constantinople, took an over-zealous part in refuting the heresies of Nestorius, and hence was led to the opposite extreme. He wandered far from the truth, and thus became the originator of the heresy which was named after him, "Eutychianism" or from its principal error, "Monophysitism" (meaning "one nature"). Eutyches taught that there was only one nature in our Lord Jesus Christ, that after the Incarnation his divine nature absorbed his human nature. He professed to base his heterodox views (though wrongfully) on the teaching of St. Cyril.

So weak is human reason that in trying to escape from one error, it rushes headlong into another. Only the infallible Church of God, because it is visibly guided by the Holy Spirit, condemns all errors, and is affected by none. Nestorius divided the one person of our divine Lord, while Eutyches confused his two natures. It was unfortunate that St. Cyril of Alexandria was then dead, and that his archdeacon Dioscorus had succeeded him as Bishop of Alexandria.

Author of the Heresy

The heresiarch Eutyches at first developed his views to a few friends in private conversation; then he proceeded to teach these heretical innovations to his subjects in his monastery. His friends used their utmost efforts to reclaim him from his errors; but they did so in vain. Eutyches displayed the inflexible obstinacy common to all heretics. Dioscorus of Alexandria supported the views of Eutyches who also gained considerable favor with Emperor Theodosius II through the court chamberlain Chrysaphius. As soon as his teaching became generally known, Eutyches was opposed by Archbishop Domnus of Antioch, Bishop Eusebius of Dorylaeum, and Patriarch Flavian of Constantinople who, on November 8, 448, having exhausted all means of persuasion, called together the bishops who happened to be in Constantinople, and cited the innovator to appear before the synod. Eutyches did not appear, but persisted in his private fancies and errors. He was deprived of the office of superior in the monastery, and was excommunicated by the 28 bishops, who with Flavian pronounced the sentence on November 22, 448.

Eutyches protested against the sentence of the synod, and appealed to Pope St. Leo I and to St. Peter Chrysologus of Ravenna. The latter answered him by saying: "In all things we exhort thee to attend obediently to all that is written by the most blessed Pope of Rome; for the Blessed Peter, who lives and presides in his own See, gives to seekers the truth of faith." In his appeal to the Pope, Eutyches says that he seeks refuge under the defender of religion, because he has been unjustly deprived of his rights, although he confessed the Nicene Creed. He petitioned the Pope to pronounce sentence on his faith, to forbid that he be calumniated or excluded from communion, when he had lived in continence and chastity for the last seventy years.

As Flavian had not written to the Pontiff concerning the decision of the Synod of Constantinople, Pope Leo applied to that prelate for information. Flavian answered immediately, and enclosed in his letter the acts of the synod which had condemned Eutyches. In answer to this letter the Pope sent the celebrated *Dogmatic Epistle* dated June 13, 449, in which the Catholic doctrine of the two natures of Christ, the human and divine, is expounded with masterly theological precision.

Before this famous document arrived in Constantinople, Eutyches and his friends had already taken steps to prevail upon Emperor Theodosius II to convoke a great council in Ephesus in August 449 for the examination of his case. Dioscorus was to preside at the council. Those bishops who had condemned Eutyches at Constantinople were to be deprived of their votes in the council. Pope Leo was also invited to attend, or at least to send legates to represent him.

The synod opened on August 8, 449, in the church dedicated to the Blessed Mother of God, where eighteen years previously, the great Ecumenical Council of Ephesus had been opened under the presidency of St. Cyril of Alexandria. Some 130 bishops attended this synod. The rights of the legates of the Holy See were peremptorily and summarily set aside by Dioscorus, who, acting under pressure of the synod, deposed Flavian of Constantinople and Eusebius of Dorylaeum, declared Eutyches orthodox in his teachings and re-instated him as superior of the monastery. When some of the bishops threw themselves suppliantly at the feet of Dioscorus to intercede for Flavian, the Emperor's soldiers and monks fell upon them with blows. A scene of horror ensued; the papal legates protested; one of them, Hilarus, escaped and reported the whole matter to Rome. So severely was Flavian wounded in the embroglio that he died within a few days while he was being carried into exile. From this epitome of facts we may gather why Pope Leo styled this assemblage "the Robber Synod of Ephesus." The entire Oriental Church was in the greatest confusion. Pope Leo saved it, for he was the staunch defender of truth and persecuted innocence. In October 449 he annulled all the acts of the synod. Theodosius II, however, forgot himself so in his friendship for Eutyches that he confirmed the acts of this "Robber Synod," to the great dismay and horror of the orthodox Church.

On July 28, 450, Theodosius II died suddenly, and Pulcheria, his sister, who had been co-regent with him, now became Empress. She gave her hand in marriage to Marcian, a general in the imperial army, under the condition that he would respect her vow of virginity. Acceding to her request, the marriage was celebrated, and Marcian became Emperor of the East. Both Emperor and Empress were eager to restore peace to the Church. They recalled the exiled bishops, and brought back the remains of Flavian for an honorable interment in the Church of the Apostles in Constantinople. Marcian announced his accession to the throne to Pope Leo, recommended his reign to the prayers of the Pontiff, and asked the Pope to convoke a general council, in order to heal the wounds of the Church. The Emperor and Empress sent the Pope a consoling report of their achievements, and invited him to a general council. The Pope was highly pleased with their report, but he objected to the convocation of a council, at least for the time, because the doctrine of the Church was clearly defined in his *Dogmatic Epistle,* and because the orthodox bishops had been restored to their Sees, and the guilty parties showed repentance.

But before this letter of Pope Leo arrived in Constantinople, June 9, Marcian had already issued an edict, dated May 17, 451, calling together a general council, to be held at Nicaea on September 1, 451. Thereupon the Pope acquiesced to the Emperor's edict, and appointed the bishops Lucentius and Paschasinus, and the priests Basilius and Boniface as his legates. Paschasinus was to preside at the council in the name of the Pontiff.

The council, originally scheduled for Nicaea, was transferred to Chalcedon, because the Emperor wished to be present at the sessions.

Proceedings of the Council

Opening of the Council. The council was solemnly opened on October 8, 451, in the church dedicated to St. Euphemia. Never before nor since was there such a great number of bishops present at an ecumenical council held in the Orient, for the attendance ranged from 520 to 630.

First Session (October 8, 451). By order of the papal legates it was decided that Dioscorus could not sit in the council as a synodal judge. The acts of the "Robber Synod" were read; Flavian and Eusebius were vindicated from the charges which the "Robber Synod" had unjustly brought against them. The same punishment was decreed against the leaders of the "Robber Synod" as they had meted out to their victims. Dioscorus of Alexandria, Juvenal of Jerusalem and four other bishops were deposed. The session had lasted through the day till late in the evening.

Second Session (October 10, 451). The Creeds of Nicaea and Constantinople were read; also the two synodical epistles of St. Cyril and the *Dogmatic Epistle* of Pope Leo to Flavian, which the bishops received with the joyous acclamation: "Peter has spoken through Leo."

Third Session (October 13, 451). By order of the papal legates the accusations which were made by Eusebius of Dorylaeum against Dioscorus were read. Thrice summoned to appear and defend himself, the culprit refused to obey. Then the papal legates pronounced sentence against him because he had received Eutyches into communion, prevented the reading of the *Dogmatic Epistle* of Leo at the "Robber Synod" and dared to excommunicate Pope Leo. "Hence," they said, "by us and through the present Holy Synod, the Most Holy and Most Blessed Leo, Bishop of Rome, together with the thrice Blessed Apostle Peter, who is the rock and foundation of the Catholic Church, and the basis of the right Faith, has deprived Dioscorus of his bishopric and degraded him from all sacerdotal dignity."

Fourth Session (October 17, 451). The papal legates demanded of the fathers of the council the unconditional acceptance of Pope Leo's *Dogmatic Epistle*. When 13 bishops of Egypt asked for an extension of time for acceptance until a new Patriarch of Alexandria could be appointed, the synod became indignant, and stated unequivocally that 13 bishops cannot oppose the universal belief and the authority of a synod of 600 bishops. Then a large number of abbots and monks, who favored Eutyches, presented a petition to the synod to ask for an impartial trial. When they were asked to subscribe to the *Dogmatic Epistle,* the monks refused, and threatened to withdraw from the communion of those bishops who voted contrary to their will as expressed in the petition. The synod gave them an extension of time until November 15. Then all were obliged to subscribe to the Epistle or be deposed and deprived of all dignity.

Fifth Session (October 22, 451). A profession of faith, composed by Anatolius, Bishop of Constantinople, was read, but the papal legates objected to certain parts of it. These were then corrected, in order to be in harmony with the doctrinal expressions of the *Dogmatic Epistle* of Leo. The definition in the Creed reads: Ἐκδιδάσκομεν ἕνα καὶ τὸν αὐτὸν Χριστὸν υἱὸν κύριον μονογενῆ ἐκ δύο φύσεσιν ἀσυγχύτως, ἀτρέπτως, ἀδιαιρέτως, ἀχωρίστως γνωρι ζόμενον. "We teach that one and the same Christ, the Lord, the only begotten Son consists of two natures, without confusion, without change, without separation, without division." This formula was accepted by all the members of the council.

Sixth Session (October 25, 451). Both Marcian and Pulcheria were present at this session. The Emperor offered certain decrees to the council, and recommended their acceptance. The decrees, which were later formulated into canons, forbade monks to build monasteries without the consent of the bishop; clerics were forbidden to engage in secular business, and to pass from one diocese into another of their own free will.

The principal work of the council came to an end in this session. The bishops asked for permission to go home, but Marcian wished them to remain a few days more, to expedite business of a secondary importance.

Seventh and Eighth Sessions (October 26, 451). A controversy pertaining to jurisdiction which had arisen between Maximus of Antioch and Juvenal of Jerusalem, was amicably adjusted. Theodoret anathematized Nestorius and Eutyches, and was reinstated as Bishop of Cyrus.

Ninth Session (October 27, 451). The case of Ibas, Bishop of Edessa, who had been deposed by the "Robber Synod," was examined.

Tenth Session (October 28, 451). Bishop Ibas was reinstated as Bishop of Edessa.

Eleventh Session (October 29, 451). The case of Bassian, former Bishop of Ephesus, was considered.

Twelfth and Thirteenth Sessions (October 30, 451). The council ordained that a new bishop should be elected for Ephesus, and that Bassian and Stephen, to alleviate their needs, should be re-imbursed from the church property. The bishops settled the dispute between Eunomius of Nicomedia and Anastasius of Nicaea by deciding that Nicaea was the ecclesiastical metropolis in Bithynia, and enjoys privileges and exemptions only in civil matters.

Fourteenth Session (October 31, 451). The case of Bishop Sabinian of Perrha was examined. If found innocent of the charges brought against him, the council decided that he should be re-instated in his bishopric.

Fifteenth Session (October 31, 451). The papal legates were absent from this session in which the thirty canons were compiled.

Sixteenth Session (November 1, 451). The occasion for this session was the controversy raised by the famous Canon 28. The papal legates protested strongly against this canon, because it gave to the Bishop of Constantinople the first rank in the Universal Church after the Bishop of Rome. The protest of the papal legates was duly recorded in the acts of the council. With this session the Council of Chalcedon, which had lasted three weeks, came to an end.

To the acts of the council the bishops attached an explanatory document which the legates bore to Rome. In this document the bishops asked Pope Leo for confirmation of the acts of the council.

Bishop Anatolius of Constantinople and Emperor Marcian wrote to Pope Leo, to ask for confirmation of the acts, especially of the protested Canon 28.

Pope Leo replied to the Emperor's letter on May 22, 452, and thanked him for the interest he had taken in restoring peace in the Church; but he sternly rejected Canon 28. On the same day, the Pope answered Anatolius, praised him for his return to the true faith, reprimanded him, however, for his pride and ambition, and exhorted him to practise humility. Under the same date, Pope Leo also wrote to Pulcheria, to give expression of his regard for the Empress, but stated again in plain words that he rejected Canon 28.

Marcian issued four edicts, February 7, 452, March 13, 452, July 6, 452, July 28, 452, respectively; the first demanded the acceptance of the profession of faith of Chalcedon; the second forbade under penalties all discussions on the profession of faith; the third revoked the confirmation of the "Robber Synod," given by his predecessor, Theodosius II; the fourth set forth the civil penalties to be inflicted on all followers of Eutyches, namely, they were forbidden to make a will; they could not enlist in the army; those who live with Eutyches in his "barn" (the house could not be called a monastery) must be driven out of the Roman Empire; the writings of Eutyches and his adherents must be burned, etc. Eutyches and Dioscorus were sent into exile.

Because a rumor spread in Palestine and Egypt that Pope Leo had rejected the acts of the Council of Chalcedon, Marcian asked again in a letter to Pope

Leo, dated February 15, 453, for a formal confirmation of the council. On March 21, 453 Pope Leo issued a circular letter to all the bishops who had attended the Council of Chalcedon, confirming the profession of faith of the council and its acts, excepting, however, Canon 28. This council has always been reckoned among the ecumenical councils of the Church.

V
THE FIFTH ECUMENICAL COUNCIL
HELD AT CONSTANTINOPLE IN 553

WORK OF THE COUNCIL: Condemnation of the "Three Chapters."

While the Roman Empire in the West was breaking up beneath the blows of barbarian invasion, in the East it continued to exist, with Constantinople as its capital. Emperor Leo I, the successor of Marcian, who had displayed such zeal for the Catholic Faith at the Council of Chalcedon, followed his predecessor's example and issued several laws favorable to the interests of the Church. He confirmed the privileges enjoyed by hospitals, monasteries and ecclesiastics, and forbade that judicial business be conducted and public spectacles be staged on Sundays and feast days. Zeno, his successor, did little but embroil religious questions. Justin I not only promoted the temporal welfare of his subjects, but protected the Catholic Faith from the renewed assaults of the Eutychians. This sect had raised its head in Egypt, and had committed many acts of violence. Its partisans were too numerous, and too well supported by those in authority, to be successfully put down. Their one great aim was to discredit the authority of the Council of Chalcedon, which had condemned them. Justinian, the son of Justin, was raised to the throne in 527, and during his reign the heretics pursued their ends with great adroitness.

A controversy arose, which had long agitated the Eastern Church, and which is now known in history as that of the "Three Chapters," the name taken from the three subjects which formed the matter of the dispute. In the days of Nestorianism certain treatises had appeared, which approved of that heresy, namely, the dissertation of Theodoret, Bishop of Cyrus, against St. Cyril; the letter of Ibas, Bishop of Edessa; and the writings of Theodore of Mopsuestia. All these works were indeed heretical; but their authors (at least the first two) retracted their errors by making an orthodox profession of faith at Chalcedon. The fathers of the Council of Chalcedon, because they were not assembled formally to examine the "Three Chapters," passed them over in silence, and demanded only that their authors should anathematize Nestorius. Theodoret and Ibas complied with this demand, while Theodore had been summoned to give an account of his faith to the Supreme Judge; he died in 428. The council, therefore, recognized the two bishops as orthodox Catholics, and did not pronounce judgment on their writings.

Now the Eutychians made this silence a ground for accusation against the Council of Chalcedon. By their repeated entreaties they induced Emperor Justinian to condemn the *"Three Chapters."* Although the Catholics knew that the writings contained errors, they feared that their express condemnation would injure the authority of the Council of Chalcedon, and afford a seeming triumph to the Eutychians. The dispute was carried on with intense animosity.

Emperor Justinian called Pope Vigilius to Constantinople. In the hope of restoring peace to the Church, the Pope set out for Constantinople. He arrived there on January 25, 547, and was received by the people with the greatest enthusiasm. Soon, however, things took another turn. The Emperor obtained from the Pope permission to discuss the *"Three Chapters"* in a synod of 70 bishops. Because there was little harmony among the bishops, Pope Vigilius reserved the judgment of the question to himself. He issued a decree, styled *Judicatum*, on April 11, 548. In this document he condemned the "Three Chapters," namely: (1) *The writings and the person of Theodore of Mopsuestia;* (2) *the letter of Ibas to Maris;* (3) *the writings of Theodoret of Cyrus,* "saving in all things the respect due to the Council of Chalcedon." Far from being a harbinger of peace, as Pope Vigilius had fondly hoped, this *Judicatum* proved to be the cause of strife. The judgment satisfied neither party in the dispute, and violent commotions arose. Throughout the West the Pontiff was accused of failing to respect the decrees of Chalcedon.

In such a state of affairs, both Pope and Emperor deemed a general council necessary; accordingly they sent letters to the principal sees of all provinces, to convoke a council to Constantinople. Very few of the Western bishops seemed willing to attend the council, and as the Pope was averse to taking any decided action in their absence, a new trouble arose. The Emperor issued a condemnatory edict of the *"Three Chapters"* and ordered it to be placarded in various churches. When the Pope heard of this high-handed proceeding, he threatened to excommunicate all who would obey the imperial edict. The Pope, then, fled to Chalcedon. During his exile he was consoled by signal proofs of respect, which were inspired by the dignity and authority vested in the Vicar of Christ. The bishops returned to their allegiance and begged pardon for their remissness, and the Emperor withdrew his edict. The Pope returned to Constantinople, and consented to the convocation of a general council, provided that the East and West, be equally represented. The Western bishops did not come, for they mistrusted Emperor Justinian. The council assembled without them.

Proceedings of the Council

Opening of the Council. Complying with the command of the Emperor, but without the consent of the Pope, the bishops opened the council on May 5, 553, under the presidency of Eutychius, Patriarch of Constantinople.

First Session (May 5, 553). At this session 151 bishops were present. A letter of the Emperor addressed to the fathers of the synod, and also the letters exchanged between the Pope and Eutychius were read. The synod sent a delegation of the three patriarchs of the East to Pope Vigilius, to invite him to attend the council.

Second Session (May 8, 553). The three patriarchs reported to the synod that the Pope refused to attend the council. The Emperor was notified of the Pope's refusal.

Third Session (May 9, 553). The acts of the preceding session were read. A profession of faith was composed, which declared adherence to the four preceding councils.

Fourth Session (May 12, 553). In this session 71 propositions, taken from the heretical writings of Theodore of Mopsuestia, were read and again condemned.

Fifth Session (May 17, 553). The council continued the examination of the heretical writings of Theodore, and the writings of Theodoret of Cyrus were also examined.

Sixth Session (May 19, 553). This session busied itself with an examination of the letter written by Bishop Ibas of Edessa to the Persian Mans. The letter was condemned as openly heretical.

While these sessions of the council were in progress, Pope Vigilius compiled a famous document, known as *Constitutum,* dated May 14, 553, signed by himself and 16 bishops and 3 Roman clerics. In this document the Pope condemned 80 heretical propositions taken from the writings of Theodore of Mopsuestia (almost identical with those of the fourth session), and repudiated in five anathemas the Christological errors of Theodore, the Pope forbade, however, to condemn his person. He also stopped further discussion of the writings of Theodoret and Ibas. This document, sent to the Emperor to be delivered to the council, was never delivered. In fact, the Emperor never accepted it.

Seventh Session (May 26, 553). Various documents, such as the letter of Vigilius to the Emperor and Empress, the promise of Vigilius to anathematize the "Three Chapters," if his decree *Judicatum* were restored to him, were read. Finally an edict of the Emperor was read, which commanded the bishops to strike out the name of Vigilius in the diptychs of the Church, "without any prejudice, however, to communion with the Apostolic See." This imperial edict was published on July 14, 553.

Eighth Session (June 2, 553). In this session were *anathematized*: (1) the writings and the person of Theodore of Mopsuestia; (2) the writings of Theodoret of Cyrus; (3) the letter of Ibas, Bishop of Edessa to Mans. The condemnations were summed up in 14 anathemas.

The acts of the council were signed by 164 bishops, of whom eight were African.

Pope Vigilius, together with other Latin bishops, was banished. The Roman clergy and people, however, petitioned the Emperor to permit the return of the Pope. The Emperor consented on the condition that Vigilius would recognize the council, and Vigilius agreed to do this. In two documents (in a letter to Eutychius of Constantinople, dated December 8, 553, and in a second *"Constitutum,"* dated February 23, 554, probably addressed to the Western bishops), the Pope condemned the "Three Chapters," without making any mention of the council.

After an absence of seven years, Vigilius set out for Rome, but died on the way at Syracuse in Sicily, June 7, 555.

In the West, in spite of the recognition of the council by Pope Pelagius I (550–560) and Gregory the Great (590–604), the Fifth Ecumenical Council acquired only gradually in public opinion an ecumenical character. In Northern Italy, Milan and Aquileja broke off communion with the Apostolic See; the former yielded only towards the end of the sixth century, whereas the latter protracted its resistance to about the year 700.

It is to be observed that throughout this controversy no doctrine of Faith was at issue. On this both parties agree, Pope and Bishops, the East and the West alike. The question was whether, in the present state of the Church, it was prudent to condemn those writings which the Council of Chalcedon had not condemned, and to excommunicate a man whom the council had not anathematized. The question, thus, was one of prudence, and not of Faith. The Pope changed his measures when circumstances were altered. He deemed one mode of action advisable at one time, and when conditions changed, he adopted another. Here, also, we may note the sovereign power claimed and exercised by the Church of examining suspected writings, of condemning errors, and of requiring the faithful to submit to her judgment. This authority is essentially necessary for the Catholic Church, the guardian of truth.

VI
THE SIXTH ECUMENICAL COUNCIL
HELD AT CONSTANTINOPLE IN 680

WORK OF THE COUNCIL: Condemnation of the heresy of the Monothelites.

Monophysitism having been condemned, the subtle Greeks devised another heresy, or better, revived in a new form the heresy of Eutyches, with some modifications. They taught that there was but one will and operation in our divine Lord; hence their name "Monothelites" or "asserters of one will." On the other hand, as the Catholic Church maintains that there are two distinct, though inseparable, natures in her divine Founder, she also holds that there are two distinct wills—the divine and the human will—in Christ, which can never conflict with each other, yet can never be confused one with the other. The error of the Monothelites was vehemently and obstinately proposed by Sergius, Patriarch of Constantinople. He intruded himself craftily into the good graces of Emperor Heraclius (610–641), who supported him in his heretical stand by the celebrated edict, called *Ekthesis* (Exposition), which was composed by Sergius. St. Sophronius, monk, later Patriarch of Jerusalem, perceived the magnitude of the evil. He published a treatise in which, after he had established on solid scriptural foundations the distinction of the two natures in Christ, he laid down the constant doctrine of the Church in regard to the two wills and operations in Christ.

AUTHOR OF THE HERESY

Sergius, Patriarch of Constantinople, wrote a letter to Pope Honorius I (625–638) in the hope of extorting from him some reply which would seem to favor his heretical views. His letter was one of artful dissimulation and crafty deceit. Suppressing the role which he really acted, he pretended in all simplicity to consult the Pope concerning a doctrinal difficulty which might be the occasion of scandal. He employed theological terms calculated to mislead the Pontiff, and to obscure the true question at issue. The reply of Pope Honorius was in thorough accord with the interpretation in which he understood the cunning letter of the heretic. If Honorius was deceived by Sergius, the reason was that being honest, practical and straightforward, he thought that the wily Greek had sought his advice in the same spirit. It never entered into his mind that the plain letter which seemed to ask for guidance, was a cunningly devised trap to inveigle him, at least, into ambiguous language, on the theological question whether there were one or two wills in Christ.

Honorius replied to Sergius in 634. After praising his wish to preserve silence in relation to a new phrase which might scandalize the simple, he emphasized the *defined* truth of two complete natures in Christ. He inferred that the will of our Lord was but one, because he assumed a perfect human nature, one created before the existence of sin, and therefore in perfect harmony, excluding all contrariety to the divine Will. Whether "on account of the operations of the divinity and humanity we ought to speak of one or two energies," is to be left to the grammarians to decide. A second letter of Honorius, of which a fragment is extant, brings out the same thought which he expressed in the first. In neither letter did Honorius teach any heresy.

During the lifetime of Honorius, Sergius would not publish the letters which the Pope had addressed to him. Evidently he must have believed that Honorius did not support his heretical views, but rather contradicted them in a most uncompromising and formidable manner.

After the death of Honorius (638) Sergius induced Emperor Heraclius to publish his famous edict *Ekthesis*.

The immediate successors of Pope Honorius do not consider Honorius a heretic. On the contrary they defend him. Pope John IV (640–642) assured the Emperor that the whole West was scandalized by the attempt which Pyrrhus, Patriarch of Constantinople, was then making to give sanction to the new heresy by connecting the authority of Honorius with it. He denied that his predecessor had any thought of giving approval to the Monothelite doctrine, and he begged the Emperor to withdraw the *Ekthesis* which he had forced the bishops to sign.

Both the heresy and the imperial edict were condemned by Pope Severinus, who succeeded Honorius, and by St. Martin I (649–655), whose zeal for truth cost him both his liberty and his life. Emperor Constans II (641–668), successor of Heraclius, issued a second edict, called *Typus* in favor of the Monothelites, and then seized the Pope. The Holy Father was put in chains, led off to Constantinople and treated with contempt and barbarity. After ninety-three days of intolerable imprisonment he was sent into exile. Within two years, on September 16, 655, he died from the hardships which he had suffered in captivity.

Emperor Constantine Pogonatus (668–685) resolved to attempt the pacification of the troubled Church by holding a general council. To this end he wrote to Pope Donus on August 12, 678, to request his concurrence in his plans. When the letter of the Emperor arrived in Rome, Pope Agatho had already succeeded Donus. Agatho concurred with the plan of the Emperor without delay, and began preparations at once. He wished for the Western Church to pronounce its judgment on the question at issue, and he, therefore, ordered that synods be held in various parts of the West. We read that synods were held at Milan, at Heathfield in England, and at Rome, in which latter place 125 bishops assembled under Pope Agatho. In all these synods Monothelitism was condemned.

The Pope appointed as legates to the council: the bishops Abundantius of Paterno, John of Reggio and John of Porto, the priests Theodore and George, the deacon John and the subdeacon Constantine of Rome, and the priest Theodore of Ravenna. He gave two highly important documents to the legates to take to Constantinople; one was the *Dogmatic Epistle* of Pope Agatho in which three points stand out very prominently: (1) the precision and clearness in which Pope

Agatho states the Catholic doctrine on the two wills in Christ; (2) the firmness with which he repeatedly declares the infallibility of the Roman Church; (3) the pronounced assurance that all his predecessors had held fast to the Catholic doctrine, and had no thought of accusing Honorius of heresy. The second document was the synodical epistle of the Roman Synod, which was signed by the Pope and 125 bishops.

On the arrival of the papal legates in Constantinople on September, 10, 680, the Emperor addressed an edict to George, Patriarch of Constantinople and to the other patriarchs, inviting them and their suffragan bishops to attend the council. The papal legates were received enthusiastically and were lodged in the Placidia Palace.

Proceedings of the Council

Opening of the Council. The council was held in a hall of the Imperial Palace, known by the name "Trullus," because it was surmounted by a cupola or dome. It opened under the presidency of the papal legates and the honorary presidency of the Emperor who was present at the first eleven sessions, and at the last, on November 7, 680.

First Session (November 7, 680). It seems that only 43 bishops or procurators were present. The papal legates demanded in an allocution to the Emperor that the representatives of the Constantinopolitan Church should describe the origin of the innovation which had disturbed the peace of the Church for the last 46 years. Macarius of Antioch and his followers declared: "We have not invented new terms, we teach what we have received from the Ecumenical Councils, from the Holy Fathers, from Sergius, Honorius, and others, and we are ready to prove this." Then the acts of the Council of Ephesus were read, but nothing which could even be construed as favoring Monothelitism, could be shown.

Second Session (November 10, 680). The acts of the Council of Chalcedon were read, and were, of course, unfavorable to the heresy. Macarius was definitively refuted by Pope St. Leo's *Dogmatic Epistle.*

Third Session (November 13, 680). A letter of Mennas to Pope Vigilius, and two supposed letters of Vigilius were rejected as obvious interpolations. Macarius, unable to substantiate Monothelitism from the acts of the previous councils, was ordered to prove that his assertions were taken from the writings of the Fathers.

Fourth Session (November 16, 680). The *Dogmatic Epistle* of Pope Agatho was read, and received with tremendous acclamations by the fathers of the council.

Fifth Session (December 7, 680). Macarius and his friends delivered two volumes of passages taken from the writings of the Fathers, which they thought favored Monothelitism.

Sixth Session (February 12, 681). The papal legates declared that the testimonies of the Fathers, quoted by Macarius, had been deliberately falsified.

Seventh Session (February 13, 681). The Roman collection of passages, taken from the writings of the Fathers, testifying to two wills and two operations in Christ, were read. Macarius, however, remained obstinate.

Eighth Session (March 7, 681). Patriarch George of Constantinople and all his suffragans declared that they accepted the definition of Pope Agatho. Macarius was, then, asked whether he admitted two wills and two operations in Christ, and he answered that he would not admit them, "even if he were cut limb from limb, and thrown into the sea."

Ninth Session (March 8, 681). Macarius was deposed as patriarch.

Tenth Session (March 18, 681). The Roman collection of passages from the Fathers was found to agree with the original Greek codices.

Eleventh Session (March 20, 681). The treatise of Sophronius, addressed to Sergius, was read. The Emperor stated that he was unable to take part in the following sessions on account of urgent imperial business.

Twelfth Session (March 22, 681). A series of documents which Macarius had delivered to the Emperor, the letter of Sergius to Honorius, and the latter's reply were read.

Thirteenth Session (March 28, 681). The originators and leaders of Monothelitism, Sergius of Constantinople, Cyrus of Alexandria, Pyrrhus, Peter and Paul of Constantinople, were anathematized in this session. The fathers of the council added: "We have also decreed to eject from the Holy Catholic Church of God, and to anathematize Honorius, who was Pope of ancient Rome, because we find from the writings he gave to Sergius, that in all things he held the latter's view, and confirmed the impious dogmas."

Fourteenth Session (April 5, 681). The interpolations of the acts of the Fifth Ecumenical Council and the fictitious letters of Pope Vigilius were anathematized.

Fifteenth Session (April 26, 681). Polychronius, a priest and monk, promised to restore a dead man to life as an act of divine confirmation of Monothelitism. The fathers of the council witnessed the farce from a window; Polychronius failed to work the miracle. He was asked to renounce the heresy. When he refused to do so, he was anathematized.

Sixteenth Session (August 9, 681). The Syrian priest Constantine of Apamea advanced a new theory of the two wills of Christ, obviously heretical. It was immediately rejected by the council.

Seventeenth Session (September 11, 681). A profession of faith was considered, composed, and accepted by the council. It reads as follows: Δύο δὲ φυσικὰς ἐνεργείας ἀδιαιρέτως, ἀτρέπτως, ἀμερίστως, ἀσυγχύτως ἐν αὐτῷ τῷ κυρίῳ ἡμῶν Ἰησοῦ Χριστῷ τῷ ἀληθινῷ θεῷ ἡμῶν δοξάζομεν, τουτέστι θείαν ἐνέργειαν καὶ ἀνθρωπίνην ἐνέργειαν κατὰ τὸν θεηγόρον Λέοντα.

"We proclaim two natural operations in our Lord Jesus Christ, our true God, undivided, unchangeable, without confusion, without separation, that is, a divine operation and a human operation, according to the divine preacher Leo."

Eighteenth Session (September 16, 681). Emperor Constantine Pogonatus was present. In this session anathema was pronounced over all who had taught

Monothelitism. In the condemnations Pope Honorius was mentioned by name.

The decrees of the council were signed by the papal legates, by 174 bishops and procurators, and by the Emperor. The council requested Pope Agatho to confirm the acts. Pope Agatho died on January 10, 682. The news of his death and the election of his successor reached Constantinople before the papal legates had departed for Rome.

Pope St. Leo II (682–683), successor of St. Agatho, gave the requested confirmation of the acts of the council in 683 with an important correction, however, of the condemnation of Honorius, who was condemned (in the confirmation of the acts) "because he did not illuminate this Apostolic Church with the teaching of the Apostolic tradition, but by profane treachery *'permitted'* its purity to be polluted." The famous historian Grisar holds the opinion that by these words Leo II explicitly abrogated the condemnation of Honorius for heresy, and substituted a *"condemnation of his negligence."*

A Word on Pope Honorius.—The writer of the article on Honorius in the *Catholic Encyclopedia*, Vol. vii, page 455, says that *"no Catholic has the right to defend Honorius."* The writer of the present book does not agree with this assertion. Such great Church historians as Grisar, Hergenroether, Mann, Alzog, and others, have *defended* Honorius. And his immediate successors in the Apostolic Chair did not censure him.

Honorius had been warned by St. Gregory the Great, his teacher, to be extremely careful and cautious when he dealt with the wily Greeks. Following this advice, Honorius was of the opinion that to rush precipitately into this new controversy would bring about untold harm; hence, he hesitated. Honorius was simply silent on defining the question at issue. Later developments of the controversy show that his silence was imprudent. Hence, the fault which Honorius committed was one only of imprudent silence. In subsequent centuries the Holy See has imposed silence when important questions came up. In the controversy on Grace between the Molinists and Thomists (1607), in the controversy on the Immaculate Conception in the sixteenth century (St. Pius V) silence was imposed. No harm was seen in these injunctions. Why so much ado in the case of Honorius? The *Dogmatic Epistle* of Pope Agatho stated clearly the Catholic doctrine on the two wills and operations in Christ. The Pope says that thus he received it from his predecessors. Now, Honorius was one of his predecessors. And Pope Agatho continues: "Hence, when the Patriarchs of Constantinople endeavored to introduce heretical novelties into Christ's unspotted Church, my predecessors never ceased to exhort them to desist from their errors, at least, by *maintaining silence*." This is a clear allusion to the conduct of Pope Honorius. St. Agatho then mentions the names of those who should be anathematized by the Council. *Honorius is not on the list.* Hence, he was vindicated by St. Agatho. The condemnation of Honorius by the Council of Constantinople was a contradiction of the sentiment expressed in the fourth session, in which the bishops declared that Peter had spoken through Agatho, and that the See of Rome was the Rock of Faith. Pope St.

Leo II, confirming the acts of the council, made a distinction and correction in the case of Honorius, when he came to pronounce anathema on the Monothelites. The ever-present fear of an Eastern schism may have influenced Leo II not to withdraw the name of Honorius from the list. As long as he had made a distinction in the condemnation—and it was a strong one—he believed he had settled the question satisfactorily. To some extent spite and jealousy, apparent before and after the council, prompted the condemnation of Honorius by the council. The vital Honorius question was greatly discussed and *thoroughly examined* at the Vatican Council (1870); but all findings, objections, heated debates and proud opposition could not dim the one, great, consoling, and all-important word of Jesus Christ: "Thou art Peter, and upon this rock I will build *My Church*" (St. Matthew, 16:18).

VII
THE SEVENTH ECUMENICAL COUNCIL
HELD AT NICEA IN 787

WORK OF THE COUNCIL: Condemnation of Iconoclasm.

The successors of Constantine Pogonatus, during whose reign the Sixth Ecumenical Council was held, were both brutal and stupid princes. Their chief occupation was war and bloodshed. In seventy years, eight Emperors died a violent death. Then Leo III (717–741), surnamed the Isaurian, a warlike prince, obtained the throne. Other Emperors had patronized heresy, it is true, but Leo displayed to the astonished world the spectacle of an Emperor becoming the originator of a heresy, called "iconoclasm" (breaking of images). He had been born and educated in the warriors' camp. His ignorance of religion was profound, yet he indulged in his childish fancy of becoming a reformer of religion. Leo had conceived a prejudice against the use and veneration of images, and pronounced the custom of the Church idolatrous. He resolved to destroy images and statues of the saints, and began his nefarious undertaking by issuing an edict in the year 726, which commanded that all the images of Our Lord, of the Blessed Virgin, and of the saints be removed from the churches. This attempt, so opposed to the principles and practice of the universal Church, excited the indignation of the Christian world. The inhabitants of Constantinople openly expressed their discontent with the ordinances of the Emperor. Great supporters of Leo were the Bishops Constantine of Nacolia, Theodosius of Ephesus, Thomas of Claudiopolis, and the Syrian renegade Beser.

Germanus, Patriarch of Constantinople, boldly opposed the heretical innovation of the Emperor. He tried at first to enlighten the obstinate Leo in private conferences, in which he pointed out to him that the veneration bestowed on the sacred images was tendered to the person whom the images represented, just as people, honoring the portrait or statue of the Emperor, give honor to him; that this relative veneration had ever been rendered from the earliest times to the images of our Lord and His Blessed Mother, and that it was an act of impious audacity to assail a doctrine so venerable and so universal. But the conferences were in vain; the Emperor stubbornly persisted in his error.

The Patriarch referred the question to Pope St. Gregory II (715–731), who thanked him for his zeal in combating the rising error. The Pope then wrote to the Emperor, exhorted him to revoke the edict, and reminded him that he was not competent to decide such a question. The Emperor replied in the manner of men who are accustomed to wield force more readily than argument. He burnt all the sacred images in one of the public places of the city, and in the churches he whitewashed the walls, which were covered with precious paintings. He ordered that a large picture of our Lord, which had been erected by Constantine at the entrance to the palace, be smashed. Some women who happened to be on the spot implored the military officer to desist from his impious task, but their prayers were disregarded. The officer mounted a ladder, and with a hatchet hacked away the countenance of Our Lord. The women, beside themselves with grief and indignation, pulled away the ladder; the officer fell down and was killed on the spot. The women were condemned to death. The Patriarch, Germanus, was driven from his See, and died in exile in his ninetieth year.

Iconoclasm was condemned at synods held in Rome under Popes St. Gregory II and St. Gregory III (731–741), and at synods held in Jerusalem under the Patriarch, Theodore. Among the firm defenders of veneration of images of our Lord, the Blessed Mother and the saints, and of the relics of the saints, we must mention St. John Chrysorrhoas of Damascus (St. John Damascene), who composed three apologies in behalf of veneration of images. The first he wrote at the beginning of iconoclasm, the second and third after the deposition of Germanus of Constantinople.

Constantine Copronymus, the son and successor of Leo (741), followed in his father's steps; in fact, he went beyond his father's example in reckless impiety. Educated without religion, his violent character led him to persecute with savage fury those who honored the sacred images. Mutilation or death was their portion their eyes were torn out, their noses were cut off, they were cast into the river. The Emperor's rage directed itself with special violence against the monks. Their beards were steeped in pitch and set on fire and the sacred images were broken on their battered heads.

The iconoclastic persecution extended into the provinces. Servile governors made war not only upon the images of the saints, but also upon their precious relics. The vandals tore them out of the sanctuaries, they threw them into rivers and common sewers; they burnt them together with bones of animals; they deemed no outrage too gross or too revolting to be inflicted on the relics.

Copronymus went so far as to convoke a synod in Constantinople which should condemn the veneration of images, and 338 bishops assembled under the presidency of Theodosius of Ephesus. They rejected veneration of images as idolatry. The decision of this synod was published on August 27, 754.

After the death of Constantine Copronymus on September 14, 775, and that of his son, Leo IV on September 8, 780, the sovereign power devolved on Irene, regent during the minority of her son Constantine VI (Porphyrogenitus). The distressed Church now received a gleam of hope, for the Empress detested the impiety of iconoclasm. In her anxiety to heal the many wounds which her predecessors had inflicted on religion during their reigns, she consulted the Patriarch Tarasius of Constantinople, who advised her to write to Pope Hadrian I (772–795) and request him to convoke an ecumenical council to condemn iconoclasm. The Pope granted her request readily. He appointed the archpriest, Peter and the abbot Peter as his legates; they were despatched to Constantinople with letters and documents. On the arrival of the legates, Empress Irene with her son summoned the bishops to Constantinople to take part in the ecumenical council.

It was their intention to hold the council in the imperial city, but due to a hostile demonstration of the iconoclasts, it was transferred to Nicaea in Bithynia, where the First Ecumenical Council had been held in 325.

Proceedings of the Council

Opening of the Council. The council was solemnly opened on September 24, 787, in the church of St. Sophia. Three hundred and sixty-eight bishops and procurators had assembled from all parts of the empire; two imperial commissioners maintained order in the city, and the bishops were able to deliberate in peace and safety.

First Session (September 24, 787). Three bishops, Basilius of Ancyra, Theodore of Myra, and Theodosius of Amorium begged pardon for having fallen into the heresy of iconoclasm. After a solemn abjuration of the heresy they were received into the council. Seven other bishops who asked for forgiveness, were ordered to present their petition at another session.

Second Session (September 26, 787). The letters of Pope Hadrian written to Empress Irene and to Patriarch Tarasius were read. The papal legates asked Tarasius and the assembled bishops, whether they were willing to accept the doctrine of veneration of images "according to the synodical letters of the most blessed Hadrian, Pope of the older Rome," to which question the bishops of the council answered: "We follow, we receive, we admit."

Third Session (September 28, 787). Bishop Gregory of Neo-Caesarea and the bishops of Nicaea, Rhodus, Iconium, Hierapolis, Pessinum, and Karpathus, having made their abjuration, were received into the council.

Fourth Session (October 1, 787). The lawfulness of the veneration of images was proven by many passages taken from Holy Scripture and from the writings of the holy Fathers. Anathemas were pronounced over the iconoclasts.

Fifth Session (October 4, 787). It was shown that the iconoclast heresy came originally from the Jews, Saracens and Manicheans.

Sixth Session (October 6, 787). The definition of the pseudo-Seventh Council was read and condemned, chapter by chapter.

Seventh Session (October 13, 787). In this session the council issued a definition of faith, concerning the veneration of holy images, in these words:

Ὁρίζομεν σὺν ἀκριβείᾳ πάσῃ καὶ ἐμελείᾳ παρακλησίως τῷ τύπῳ τοῦ τιμίου καὶ ζωοποιοῦ σταυροῦ ἀνατίθεσθαι τὰς σεπτὰς καὶ ἁγίας εἰκόνας, τὰς ἐκ χρωμάτων καὶ ψηφίδος καὶ ἑτέρας ὕλης ἐπιτηδείως ἐχούσης, ἐν ταῖς ἁγίαις τοῦ Θεοῦ ἐκκλησίαις, ἐν ἱεροῖς σκεύεσι καὶ ἐσθῆσι, τοίχοις τὲ καὶ σανίσιν, οἴκοις τὲ καὶ ὁδοῖς· τῆς τὲ τοῦ κυρίου καὶ Θεοῦ καὶ σωτῆρος ἡμῶν Ἰησοῦ Χριστοῦ εἰκόνος, καὶ τῆς ἀχράντου δεσποίνης ἡμῶν τῆς ἁγίας Θεοτόκου, τιμίων τὲ ἀγγέλων, καὶ πάντων ἁγίων καὶ ὁσίων ἀνδρῶν. Ὅσῳ γὰρ συνεχῶς δι᾽ εἰκονικῆς ἀνατυπώσεως ὁρῶνται τοσοῦτον καὶ οἱ ταύτας θεώμενοι διανίστανται πρὸς τὴν τῶν πρωτοτύπων μνήμην τε καὶ ἐπιπόθησιν, καὶ ταύταις ἀσπασμὸν καὶ τιμητικὴν προσκύνησιν ἀπονέμειν, οὐ μὴν τὴν κατὰ πίστιν ἡμῶν ἀληθινὴν λατρείαν, ἢ πρέπει μόνῃ θείᾳ φύσει.

"We define with all certainty and diligence that as the figure of the precious and life-giving Cross, so the venerable and holy images, both painted and of stone and of other proper material, should be set up in the holy churches of God, put on the sacred vessels and vestments, on the walls and on tables, in houses and along the roads: that is, the image of our Lord God and Saviour Jesus Christ, and of our inviolate Lady, the holy Mother of God, and of the honorable angels, and of all holy and distinguished men. The more frequently they are seen by a pictorial representation, the more readily those who contemplate them, are excited to a remembrance of and desire for the prototypes, and to bestow upon them a respectful devotion; not, however, a 'latria' (adoration), which is, according to our faith, and as is becoming, bestowed upon the divine nature alone." All the bishops signed this profession of faith.

Eighth Session (October 23, 787). At the request of Empress Irene the last session of the council was held in Constantinople, in the Magnaura Palace, at which the Empress and her son were present. The profession of faith was read again; the Empress and her son signed the document.

This council also edited 22 canons for the restoration of ecclesiastical discipline.

The council then came to a close; Irene dismissed the bishops, and rewarded them with rich presents. The papal legates returned to Rome with letters from Irene, and with the acts of the council, written in Greek.

Though Hadrian I did not send a formal confirmation of the council to Constantinople and to Irene, because his just demands in connection with the restoration of the patrimonies and of his jurisdiction in the diocese of Illyricum had not been attended to, he, nevertheless, accepted the council, and ordered its acts to be translated into Latin. The faultiness of this translation caused considerable disturbance in the West, but a very lengthy letter of Hadrian I to Charlemagne solved all doubts, and finally settled the difficulty, so that the West likewise accepted this council as an ecumenical council.

VIII
THE EIGHTH ECUMENICAL COUNCIL
HELD AT CONSTANTINOPLE IN 869

WORK OF THE COUNCIL: Removal of the schism caused by Photius.

The first seeds for the separation of the Greek Church from the Latin Church and from the Apostolic See were sown by the third canon of the Council of Constantinople (381), and by the twenty-eighth canon of the Council of Chalcedon (451). The unfriendly sentiments which these canons created between Rome and Constantinople were increased by various circumstances, such as the difference of national characters, of rite, and discipline, and particularly through the despotism exercised by the Emperors of the East, and the ambition of many patriarchs of Constantinople, who found ready allies among the Eastern bishops. The relations of the Byzantine Court with the Court of the Pope became more unfriendly in view of the political changes in Italy, especially since the States of the Church had come into existence. The greatest stumbling block to unity was occasioned by the restoration of the Western Empire, which was a source of great anxiety to the rulers of the East.

Many emperors and patriarchs of Constantinople exhibited a marked aversion towards the See of Rome. The formal separation of the Eastern and Western Church, however, took place under the dissolute Emperor, Michael III (857–867), who left the government of the empire to his uncle, Bardas, a man of vicious character. Bardas hated the virtuous Ignatius, Patriarch of Constantinople. Bardas had been publicly denied Holy Communion by Ignatius on the feast of the Epiphany because of his scandalous life. He swore revenge, and conspired with Archbishop Gregory Asbestas of Syracuse against the intrepid patriarch, who was asked to force the Empress-Mother and daughters to enter the convent. When Ignatius refused to do so, he was banished to the island Terebinthos on November 23, 857, having been Patriarch of Constantinople for twelve years.

AUTHOR OF THE SCHISM

Photius, a layman, full of ambition and of a very dubious character to say the least, succeeded Ignatius as Patriarch. He received all the Orders within a week from the hands of Gregory Asbestas. A promotion so irregular scandalized the Church, and the bishops at first refused to recognize the usurper; but eventually some were won over to the cause of Photius, and the others, who dissented, were banished. Photius was anxious to have his appointment confirmed by Pope Nicholas I (858–867). For this purpose he wrote a crafty letter to the Pope to announce his election, saying that his elevation was against his wish, and that he had yielded with tears to overbearing force. He added that Ignatius had retired of his own accord to a monastery, in order to pass his last days in peaceful preparation for death. His letter was accompanied by another from the Emperor which confirmed his statements. Ignatius, meanwhile, was shut up in a loathsome prison, where he was treated with indignity. These things the Patriarch and the Emperor had carefully concealed from the Pope, but the letters created a suspicious atmosphere. Pope Nicholas declined to decide on the election of Photius without a thorough examination. He sent Bishop Rodoald of Porto and Bishop Zachary of Anagni as his legates to Constantinople, to investigate the facts of the case. On their arrival at the imperial city the legates were immediately put under surveillance and cut off from every source of information. They were also threatened with punishment, if they refused to recognize Photius as Patriarch. Although they resisted for a long time, they, at length, yielded to the will of the Emperor, having been subdued by his solicitations, promises and threats. A synod was held in May 861, at which 318 bishops were present; it deposed Ignatius. The papal legates concurred with this deceitful deal of intrigue and fraud. Photius was declared Patriarch of Constantinople.

The unhappy Patriarch Ignatius, whom Photius tried to compel by every kind of ill treatment to resign his dignity, appealed to the Pope, who gave the matter a careful examination at a synod convened in Rome (March 862). He annulled the decision of the Synod of Constantinople, and suspended Photius from all his ecclesiastical dignities. The same sentence of suspension was pronounced over the papal legates and over Gregory Asbestas.

Photius, whose cause was espoused by the Emperor, did not submit to this sentence; on the contrary, he was now bent on excommunicating the Pope. Photius, having won over to his side a great portion of the people, did not long delay the execution of his unheard-of plan. In 867 he addressed a circular to the Eastern patriarchs, in which he makes numerous complaints against the Latins, accusing them among other things of heresy. A synod was held, and excommunication and deposition were pronounced against Pope Nicholas. Only 21 bishops signed the document, but Photius forged more than a thousand signatures to this document.

The death of Emperor Michael III suddenly changed the state of affairs. Basil, his murderer, had himself proclaimed Emperor. He was anointed Emperor by Photius, from whose hands he received Holy Communion. However, on the next day, September 25, 867, the new Emperor expelled Photius from his usurped see and shut him up in the monastery of Skepe. He recalled the much-tried Ignatius immediately, and reinstated him in his dignity and office on November 23, 867, exactly ten years after he had been sent into exile by his predecessor. Emperor Basil notified Pope Nicholas of what he had done in the case of Ignatius. In a second letter to the Pope, the Emperor asked that mercy be shown to the repentant adherents of Photius, and that legates be sent to Constantinople to repair the late scandals. Ignatius also addressed himself to the Pope.

Hadrian 11(867–872), successor to Nicholas, held a synod at St. Peter's, Rome, annulled the decrees of the pseudo-council of 867, and sent three legates,

Donatus, Stephen and Marianus, to Constantinople, to preside at the Eighth Ecumenical Council. The legates entered Constantinople amid the acclamations of the people on September 25, 869, and were lodged in the Magnaura Palace.

Proceedings of the Council

Opening of the Council. The council was solemnly opened on October 5, 869, in the church of St. Sophia. To add to the solemnity of the occasion, the true Cross of Our Lord was erected in the midst of the assembly. The papal legates presided at the council.

First Session (October 5, 869). The papal legates were asked to show their credentials. As they deemed the question rather insolent, they hesitated to answer. When they were convinced that no contempt of the Apostolic See was meant by the request, but rather that this precaution was taken because of the prevarication of Rodoald and Zachary, the legates of Nicholas I, they were satisfied, and read the letter of Hadrian II to the council. The letter contained a condemnation of all heresies; an anathema against Photius; also a *Document of Reconciliation*, which stated clearly the conditions which those who had sided with Photius must fulfill, if they wished to be reconciled.

Second Session (October 7, 869). Several bishops who had joined Photius asked for pardon, and having signed the *"document of reconciliation,"* they were admitted to the council, but they were forbidden to perform any episcopal functions until the following Christmas. The time intervening they had to spend in doing penance.

Third Session (October 11, 869). The Bishops Theodulus of Ancyra and Nicephorus of Nicaea were asked to subscribe to the Roman definition; they refused. The letter of Hadrian II to Ignatius, dated June 10, 869, was read.

Fourth Session (October 13, 869). The bishops Zachary and Theophilus of the Photian faction were asked to sign the Roman definition; they declared that they had been received into communion by Pope Nicholas I. The papal legates, however, proved that the two schismatics lied, and when they stubbornly refused to sign, they were expelled from the council.

Fifth Session (October 20, 869). Photius was sent to the council by the Emperor. When asked whether he would abide by the decrees of Nicholas I and Hadrian II, he remained silent. Urged by the legates to repent, so that he might merit at least lay-communion, he answered: "My justification is not in this world." He relapsed again into obstinate silence and was dismissed from the council.

Sixth Session (October 25, 869). Emperor Basil attended the session. By this time the number of bishops attending the council had increased to 37. Even the Emperor urged the bishops who had favored Photius to yield to the decision of the Church, and exhorted them to repent. The dissenting bishops were given seven days of grace, in which to make their submission.

Seventh Session (October 29, 869). Emperor Basil attended again. Photius and Gregory were brought to the council, and asked whether they were willing to accept the papal decision. Urged by the legates to submit, Photius answered that they had more need of submission and repentance than he had. Finally, the council pronounced anathema over Photius "the courtier and invader, neophyte and tyrant, the condemned schismatic, adulterer and parricide, the inventor of lies and perverse dogmas, the new Judas and Dioscorus, anathema to all his followers and sympathizers." Gregory of Asbestas was also anathematized.

Eighth Session (November 5, 869). The Emperor was again present. All the writings of Photius against the Popes, and the acts of the pseudo-synod were thrown into the flames. Several iconoclasts were reconciled to the Church, the Emperor kissing them after their abjuration.

Ninth Session (February 12, 870). Several perjurers were introduced who, compelled by Photius and Michael III, had sworn falsely against Ignatius on the occasion of the mock trial. They confessed their crime, and anathematized Photius. They received a canonical penance of seven years: during the first two years they had to take their places among the penitents; during the next two years they could have their places among the catechumens, and moreover, they had to abstain from wine and meat, except on Sundays and feasts of Our Lord; during the last three years they could be with the faithful, but had to abstain from wine and meat on Mondays, Wednesdays and Fridays; they could, however, receive Holy Communion on the feasts of the Lord.

Tenth Session (February 28, 870). In the presence of the Emperor, the council edited 27 canons, many of which were directed against Photius. After the promulgation of the canons, the council issued a definition of faith which anathematized all heresies and condemned Photius and his followers. This document was signed by the papal legates, by the bishops and by the Emperor. Then the council issued an epistle, addressed to the bishops and the faithful, which gave them an account of the crimes committed by Photius, and a record of all the proceedings against him. Another epistle was addressed to Pope Hadrian II, which asked for confirmation of the decrees of the council, which in final analysis were practically his own.

The papal legates having left Constantinople without any protection from the Emperor, on their homeward journey fell into the hands of pirates, and were robbed. Of this Hadrian complained bitterly in a letter to the Emperor, on November 10, 871.

The West always acknowledged this council as ecumenical, but it was rejected by the Greek Church at the time of separation from the Latin Church in 1054 under the Patriarch, Michael Caerularius.

IX
THE NINTH ECUMENICAL COUNCIL
HELD AT THE LATERAN, ROME, IN 1123

WORK OF THE COUNCIL: Confirmation of the Concordat of Worms and abolition of the strife over investiture.

The tyranny exercised by the great feudal powers induced so many disorders and such relaxation of discipline, that those who should have been a source of edification to their flocks, became their scandal. Hence, the enemies of the Church have ever found in the tenth, eleventh and twelfth centuries an unfailing supply of reproaches and calumnies against her. But these scandals ought rather to strengthen than to shake our faith. Never was it more obvious that the Church was guided, not by man, but by the strong, over-ruling hand of God. Had the Church been a human institution, those centuries would have seen its destruction and its death. This remark applies also to other troubled periods in the history of the Church. The weakness and the sins of the pastors of the Church do not compromise her divine origin and mission; in times of the worst corruption there have been not only those chosen souls—few in number, but eminent in sanctity—to whom has been given the glorious title of Saints, but also multitudes whose lives were models of all Christian virtues, and a reproach to the world at large. Those who were scandalous in their conduct were so, not on account of their faith, but in spite of it. The moral teaching of the Church remained unsullied, and her Creed untouched. Her voice of rebuke and protest was ever audible amidst the tumult of violence and iniquity. Even when apparently most powerless, the Church was able, by her inherent divine energy, to heal the wounds inflicted on her.

One of the prevalent vices of the twelfth century was simony. Nowhere had it struck deeper roots than in Germany and Lombardy, although the abuse had also crept into France and England. The source of the evil was found in the tyranny of the secular power, which made ill use of the extensive patronage which it enjoyed in conferring benefices, bishoprics and abbeys on worldly prelates, and even selling episcopal sees and abbeys to the highest bidders. It was customary for the Emperor to put bishops and abbots in possession of their temporal domains by delivering to them the crosier and the ring. This was called the right of investiture. As the ring and crosier were the symbols of spiritual power, this practice of investiture became a great and mischievous abuse, which led men to imagine that the temporal ruler conferred the spiritual authority, an idea which ambitious and unscrupulous emperors took care to foster and strengthen. In some countries, immediately after the death of a bishop or abbot, his ring and crosier, the emblems of his spiritual jurisdiction, were taken to the sovereign, and retained by him until he saw fit to confer them upon another acceptable candidate.

Until the ceremony of investiture had been performed, whether the candidate was canonically elected or not, whether he was consecrated or not, no bishop or abbot could enter upon the duties of his office.

In taking a determined stand against this method of investiture, the Roman Pontiffs derogated from no legitimate right of a sovereign; they simply insisted upon the inherent and divinely accorded right of the Church to elect her own pastors.

St. Gregory VII (1073–1085) was not the first Pontiff to raise his voice against the abuse of lay investiture, although he was the first to use the axe on the root of the evil, for he decreed that the complete system of lay investiture should be abolished. He pronounced excommunication on all prelates who received investiture by means of crosier and ring from the hands of a layman. Gregory VII, one of the best and most able of a long line of Pontiffs, was determined to assert and to maintain the discipline of the Church. Towards Henry IV (1056–1106), emperor-elect of Germany, he never ceased to act as a tender father and friend, as long as the smallest hope of reclaiming him existed. But when his obstinacy became too apparent, when he even proceeded to publish with the concurrence of his creatures in the episcopacy an act of deposition against the supreme Pontiff, this holy Pope, with sorrowful regret, pronounced the sentence of excommunication against him. Excommunication in those days deprived one of all civil rights, and an excommunicated sovereign could not rule over Catholic subjects. A year and a day was, however, always granted to the ruler, before it became incumbent on his subjects to withdraw their allegiance. Henry, seeing himself abandoned by his subjects, pretended to seek reconciliation with the Pope. He crossed the Alps, and repaired to Gregory at the castle of Canossa in Lombardy. Confessing his guilt, and feigning profound humility, he touched the heart of Gregory VII, who on the fourth day of Henry's penance admitted him to reconciliation with the Church, and absolved him from the censures of the Church. Henry soon threw off his mask; he passed rapidly into Italy, and created an anti-Pope, Guibert, Archbishop of Ravenna. All his promises were now forgotten; Henry continued to invest bishops and abbots with crosier and ring.

The immediate successors of Gregory VII imitated his firmness in the matter of lay investiture. Under Henry V (1106–1125), the son of Henry IV, the question of investiture assumed a bloody aspect. Henry, at the head of an immense army, moved from Germany into Italy and caused untold harm.

By dint of his determination Pope Callistus II (1118–1124) finally succeeded in subduing the obstinate Henry V. Finding that his own German subjects were heartily sick of the long struggle with the Papacy, Henry yielded, and made overtures to Callistus. The Bishop of Spires and the Abbot of Fulda were sent to Rome. The Pope commissioned the Cardinal Bishop of Ostia, Lambert, the Cardinal Priest Saxo, and the Cardinal Deacon Gregory, to receive Henry into the Church, after he had abandoned all claim to investiture, and to accord to him the right of superintending the elections, and of giving investiture *by means of the sceptre*. The papal legates invited the Emperor and the bishops and nobles to a Diet at Worms.

Henry presented the following agreement to the Diet at Worms: "I, Henry, by the grace of God, august Emperor of the Romans, for the love of God and of the Lord Pope Callistus, and for the good of my soul, do yield to God and to His Holy Apostles, Peter and Paul, and to the Holy Catholic Church, every investiture by crosier and ring, and do grant that in all churches free election and consecration be held. I restore to the same Holy Roman Church all the possessions and regalia of Blessed Peter, which have been appropriated from the beginning of this discord until today, and which I hold; and as for those which I do not hold, I shall faithfully see that they be restored. I shall also faithfully help in the restitution of the possessions of all the other churches, of the princes and of others, both clerics and laymen; and I accord true peace to the Lord Pope Callistus, to the Holy Roman Church, and to all who are or have been on their side; and I shall faithfully aid the Holy Roman Church in all she asks of me."

On the other hand, Pope Callistus had agreed to the following concession "I, Callistus, Servant of the servants of God, do grant unto thee, beloved Son Henry, by the grace of God, august Emperor of the Romans that in thy presence be held, without simony or any violence, those elections of Bishops and Abbots of the German kingdom which belong to the kingdom, so that, if any discord shall arise between the parties, thou mayest, by the advice and judgment of the metropolitan and provincials, give countenance and aid to the deserving side. The person elected shall receive the regalia from thee *by means of the sceptre,* and he shall do what he owes to thee of right, excepting all those things which are known to belong to the Roman Church. Anyone, however, who is consecrated in other parts of the empire, shall receive from thee the regalia, *by means of sceptre,* within six months. I shall grant my aid, according to the duties of my Office, in all things of which thou mayest complain to me. I accord true peace to thee, and to all who are or have been on thy side during this discord. Given on September 23, 1122."

These two agreements were signed by both parties concerned and were promulgated at the Diet of Worms.

When Callistus had heard of the happy culmination of the Concordat, he sent congratulatory letters to Henry, dated December 23, 1122, asking him at the same time to send ambassadors to Rome, that they might represent him at the general council which was then being prepared.

Proceedings of the Council

Opening of the Council. All previous ecumenical councils, having been held in the East, were presided over by the papal legates. In the Ninth Ecumenical Council, held in the Lateran Basilica in Rome, and hence called "the First of the Lateran," Pope Callistus presided in person. According to some authorities 997 bishops and abbots attended, according to others, 500 bishops. It opened on the third Sunday in Lent, March 18, 1123.

First Session (March 18, 1123). The council confirmed the Concordat of Worms; thus it definitely restored peace between the Church and the State.

Second Session (March 27, 1123). The council issued canons for the restoration of discipline, mostly concerning investiture, and for the encouragement of the Crusades, granting a plenary indulgence to the Crusaders.

Third Session (April 6, 1123). The Pope issued a decree concerning the consecration of the Bishops of Corsica. He also canonized Bishop Conrad of Constance.

This council had given the finishing stroke to the conflict on investiture, which had raged for fifty years, and had embittered many.

X
THE TENTH ECUMENICAL COUNCIL
HELD AT THE LATERAN, ROME, IN 1139

WORK OF THE COUNCIL: Abolition of the papal schism and condemnation of the heresy of Peter of Bruys.

On the death of Honorius II the Church was thrown into confusion, not, on this occasion, by the imperious will of a German sovereign, but by the ambition either of individual members of the College of Cardinals or of their families.

Whilst Honorius was still alive, it was common knowledge that "a certain Peter was scheming to obtain the Papacy." This "certain Peter" belonged to a family of Jewish extraction which had become very powerful in Rome through the conversion of Peter's grandfather. This "certain Peter" became the future anti-Pope, Anacletus II. A monk of Cluny, Pope Paschal II had called him to Rome to make him a cardinal deacon. Calixtus II elevated him to the rank of a cardinal bishop. Having thus become one of the principal members of the Roman clergy, he was soon selected for important work. Sometimes in the performance of his important duties he was jointly commissioned with Cardinal Gregory, the future Pope Innocent II, whom Peter opposed so bitterly.

When the demise of Honorius II seemed imminent, the assembled cardinals agreed that no election should take place till after the Pope was buried. They entrusted to eight of their number the right of electing a successor to Honorius when death should leave the See of Peter vacant. Cardinal Gregory, though resisting, was elected to the Papacy and took the name of Innocent II (1130–1143).

Furious at being forestalled, Peter and his brothers, by a liberal distribution of money, got together a number of clergy, including many cardinals, and assembled in the Church of St. Mark. There amid the applause of Peter's party, the Cardinal Bishop of Porto invested Peter with the red mantle and acclaimed him Pope Anacletus II. Once proclaimed pope, Peter lost no time in endeavoring to gain possession of Rome. After much bloodshed, he succeeded in seizing both St. Peter's and the Lateran.

The position of the lawful Pope, Innocent II, became untenable. He therefore left Rome and went to France where he held synods at Liege and Rheims, thereby strengthening his position and authority.

Anacletus succeeded in gaining over to his cause Roger, Duke of Sicily, by giving him his sister's hand in marriage and by promising him the title of "King of Sicily, Calabria and Apulia." Thus won, Roger remained true to Anacletus.

As soon as the passes over the Alps were open, Innocent descended into northern Italy. He made peace between Pisa and Genoa. He entered Rome with Lothaire, who was crowned Emperor on June 4, 1133. The schism lasted till 1138, when Anacletus died suddenly on January 25, 1138. His successor was Gregory, Cardinal Priest of the Holy Apostles, elected as Victor IV. But on May

29, 1138, Victor and his supporters submitted to Innocent II and there was "great joy among the people."

With a view to removing the last traces of the schism, and to carrying on the work of reform, Innocent II summoned the bishops of Christendom to meet in Rome on Laetare Sunday, April 2, 1139, for the purpose of holding an ecumenical council. A very large number of prelates responded to the mandate of the Pope.

Proceedings of the Council

Opening of the Council. The Pope opened the Tenth Ecumenical Council, the second of the Lateran, on April 4, 1139, in the presence of about a thousand prelates: patriarchs, archbishops, bishops and abbots.

The work of the Council was threefold: (1) the removal of the consequences of the eight years' schism (2) the condemnation of the heresy of Peter of Bruys (3) the restoration of discipline.

(1) *Removal of the consequences of the eight years' schism.*
The proceedings of the council were opened by an address to the assembled bishops by the Pope, who, says the Chronicler of Morigney, "was superior to all the others in splendor of apparel, in venerableness of appearance, and in learning." "You know," Innocent said, "that Rome is the head of the world, and that from the Roman Pontiff all ecclesiastical honors are received, as though by feudal custom, and that without his permission they cannot be held lawfully." Such being the case, he pointed out the evils of a divided Papacy. He reminded the audience that, according to St. Augustine, whoever was cut off from the Catholic Faith, no matter if he think he is living will be, by the very crime of being separated from the unity of Christ, devoid of life and subject to the anger of God. The Pope continued amid the applause of the assembly: "Those then who are in this state must be dealt with severely," and so "whatever Peter (anti-Pope Anacletus II) decreed, we annul; whomsoever he exalted we degrade, and whomsoever he consecrated we desecrate and depose." Then Innocent upbraided the guilty parties by name and demanded that they surrender into his hands their crosiers, their palliums and their episcopal rings. Among those who had been treated with justice untempered by mercy was Cardinal Peter of Pisa, whom St. Bernard had brought repentant to Innocent's feet. The ordinations of Anacletus were declared null and void.

(2) *The condemnation of the heresy of Peter of Bruys.* Peter of Bruys first disseminated his errors in the province of Aries, France, about 1120. He denied that baptism was valid or useful when it was administered to a person who had not yet arrived at the use of reason. He decried churches as places for divine worship, and taught that the crucifix should be broken to pieces and burnt. He denied the real presence of Christ in the Holy Eucharist, ridiculed all sacrifices, prayers, alms offered for the dead. He rejected tradition and the authority of the Fathers. These errors were condemned by the council in the following words:

"Eos, qui religiositatis speciem simulantes, Domini corporis et sanguinis sacramentum, baptisma puerorum, sacerdotium et ceteros ecclesiasticos ordines et legitimarum damnant foedera nuptiarum, tamquam hereticos ab Ecclesia Dei pellimus et damnamus et per potestates exteras coerceri praecipimus."—"Those who, under the guise of religion, deny the sacrament of the Body and Blood of the Lord, infant baptism, priesthood and the other ecclesiastical Orders and lawful matrimony, we expel as heretics from the Church of God and condemn them, and command that they be punished by the secular powers." This condemnation is directed against Peter of Bruys and the neo-Manicheans, from whom the Albigensians sprang later. The canon is taken verbatim from the decrees of the Synod of Toulouse, which was held in the presence of Callistus II in 1119.

King Roger of Sicily was excommunicated for his opposition to the Papacy and for holding Church property illegally.

(3) *Restoration of discipline.* The council issued thirty canons to complete former decrees against simony, clerical incontinence, usury, tournaments, and the study of medicine and of civil law by clerics for the sake of enriching themselves.

The new Archbishop Theobald of Canterbury, who attended this council with five other English bishops and four abbots, received the pallium. At this council Sturmius, founder of the Benedictine Abbey at Fulda, Germany, was canonized.

XI
THE ELEVENTH ECUMENICAL COUNCIL
HELD AT THE LATERAN, ROME, IN 1179

WORK OF THE COUNCIL: Regulation of election of a Pope, and condemnation of the Albigensian Heresy.

"The man who in the Middle Ages deserved perhaps the highest tribute from the human race was Pope Alexander III. He, in a council held in the twelfth century, abolished as far as lay in his power the curse of slavery. He, in the Council of Venice, triumphed by his prudence over the violence of Emperor Barbarossa and compelled Henry II, King of England, to ask pardon of God and men for the murder of Thomas à Becket. He restored the rights of nations and curbed the passions of kings. Before his time, all Europe—save a small number of cities—was divided into two classes of men the lords of the lands, ecclesiastic and lay, and the slaves. The men of law who assisted the knights in their judgments and the bailiffs were but mere serfs by origin. If men have recovered their rights, it is chiefly to Pope Alexander that they are indebted for it; to him so many cities owe their new or recovered splendor." The writer who thus eulogizes Alexander is Voltaire, the foresworn enemy of the Papacy.

Alexander III (1159–1181) purchased, if we may so speak, the glory of such a eulogy by bearing for twenty years persecution, exile, struggle and proscription with heroic constancy and unshaken courage. His patience was equalled only by his sufferings. In opposing the tyranny of Frederick Barbarossa, Alexander became in the eyes of all Europe the avenger of wrong and the protector of the oppressed. For seventeen years this great Pope endured the most bitter persecution from the hands of Barbarossa. By intrigue and despotism the Emperor created three anti-Popes successively, thereby causing a schism which did more harm to his empire than to the Church. Eventually the Lombards formed a league against this despot and tyrant, and Alexander gave the enterprise his full support. The Lombards routed the army of Barbarossa in the battle of Legnano on May 29, 1176, and forced the Emperor to seek the peace which was afterwards concluded at Venice on August 1, 1177. Barbarossa accepted the conditions of peace submitted by Alexander III.

A like struggle had been going on between Henry II of England, and the heroic Thomas à Becket. Alexander was Thomas' protector, and on learning the news of the English prelate's atrocious murder, he shed bitter tears. He excommunicated Henry II who then came to his senses, and begged for forgiveness. The repentant King then invalidated the customs which he had unlawfully introduced into the Church in England. When Henry expiated the crime, he was given absolution by the legates of Alexander III.

The long strife which had embittered the pontificate of Alexander III produced a sad state of disorder in the Church. Working under cover of the long struggle of Alexander III with Frederick Barbarossa, the Albigensian heresy strengthened its position in southern France. The bonds of ecclesiastical discipline were loosened, and the people came to disregard the authority of the Holy See when they saw it openly opposed by the Emperor. To check these disorders and to establish a lasting peace, Alexander III in September 1178 despatched letters and legates to all parts of the Christian world to summon to Rome for the first Sunday in Lent of 1179 "the Bishops of the East and West and of all Italy." Bishops came from Spain, France, England, Ireland, Scotland, Germany, Denmark, Hungary and Palestine.

Proceedings of the Council

Opening of the Council. The council was opened on March 5, 1179 in the Lateran Basilica. Pope Alexander III presided over the council, which was attended by over three hundred bishops and a great number of abbots, making altogether about a thousand prelates. Almost all that we know from history about the work of the council and of this great assembly of Catholic prelates is that it held three sessions; on March 5th, March 7th and March 19th, or, as other historians say, on March 5, March 14 and March 22, and that at its last session it issued twenty-seven important canons. From these canons we may gather the *three reasons* for which the council was convoked.

The work of the council was (1) To remedy the evils caused by the schism of the anti-Popes; (2) To condemn the Albigensian heresy; (3) To restore ecclesiastical discipline.

(1) *Elimination of the evils caused by the schism of the anti-Popes.* To preclude the recurrence of another schism, the council issued the following decrees: "Although our predecessors issued constitutions which sufficiently guard against discord in the election of the Supreme Pontiff, the Church has frequently suffered grievous schism on account of the audacity of wicked ambition; hence, to avoid this evil we have decreed, by the advice of our brethren and with the approbation of the holy Council, to add something to those constitutions. We, therefore, decree that if by the enemy's sowing of nettles there be no full concord among the cardinals in their choice of the Pontiff, and if *two-thirds agree,* and the *other third will not yield,* but presumes to declare another Pontiff for itself, *he* shall be the *Roman Pontiff* who is *elected* and *acknowledged* by the *two-thirds.* And if any one not being able to attain his end, relies upon the nomination by one third and usurps the name of Pontiff, he and all who recognize him are excommunicated, deprived of the exercise of their order, and even Communion shall be denied to them, unless they are at the point of death. If they do not repent, let them have their lot with Dathan and Abiron, whom the earth swallowed alive. Again, if any one be chosen by *less than two-thirds,* and no better agreement can be reached, he will incur the above punishment, unless he humbly retreats." From the reign of Alexander III, the *two-thirds system* has been the norm in the papal elections.

(2) *The condemnation of the Albigensian heresy.* The Albigensian heresy was a confused conglomeration of previous heresies. The adherents of this heresy rejected all Sacraments and external worship of the Church and manifested violent hatred against the hierarchy. The Albigenses, named after the City of Albi in southern France, their stronghold and the birthplace of the heresy, were a menace to both Church and State. The council pronounced anathema on them, their defenders and their harborers "If they die in their sins, let no offering be made for them, nor burial among Christians be accorded them."

(3) *Restoration of ecclesiastical discipline.* Of the enactments, which by their practical worth reflect so much credit on this great Christian parliament, only the more important may be named here. The eighteenth canon, in favor of the poor, did the greatest honor to the Pope and his counsellors. It ran thus: "Since the Church of God, like an affectionate Mother, is bound to provide for the poor in matters that concern the body as well as in those things which redound to the profit of the soul, therefore, lest the opportunity of reading and improving be denied to the poor persons who cannot be assisted by the resources of their own parents, we command that in each cathedral church some competent benefice be assigned to a teacher, who may *gratuitously* teach the clerks of the same church as well as the *indigent scholars.*" The interests of the poor were also safeguarded by the twenty-fifth canon enacted against usurers. Even the poorest of the poor were not forgotten, and this glorious diet of Christendom could find time to think of the lepers (canon 23). The renewal of the Treuga Dei (the truce of God) was for the benefit of the poor (canon 21). For the benefit of the poor and defenceless and for the good of trade this Council decreed continual security for clerics, pilgrims, merchants and husbandmen with their cattle, and enacted that tolls were not to be increased nor imposed except by proper authority (canon 22). The twenty-fourth canon excommunicates all who furnish ammunitions of war to the Mohammedans, or become navigators on their ships. The same penalty is launched against all pirates and those who make slaves of Christians. The twenty-sixth canon excommunicates Christians who have become domestics in the service of Jews.

The Eleventh Ecumenical Council was really one of the most magnificent diets held in the Christian world.

XII
THE TWELFTH ECUMENICAL COUNCIL
HELD AT THE LATERAN, ROME, IN 1215

WORK OF THE COUNCIL: Recovery of the Holy Land, reform of discipline, condemnation of the Albigensian Heresy.

The history of the Church is the history of modern civilization. The greatness and the power of the one is always the measure of the progress of the other. The pontificate of Innocent III affords an undeniable confirmation of this statement. Never did the Papacy rule the world more visibly. The various interests of European nations, the claims of rival kings, the imperial elections, the hopes of political parties, the prayers of whole peoples, all turned to the Sovereign Pontiff, in whom was vested the supreme authority, who was the supreme arbiter of all disputes, and the universal mediator.

Raised to the Chair of St. Peter, in spite of his protestations, Innocent III (1198–1216) gave his whole mind and heart to the task which the Church had imposed on him. His tireless energy was equal to the numerous and varied occupations which called for his attention and consideration. His judgments, stamped with the zeal of solemn grandeur and impartiality, were uttered only after mature deliberation. "His love of justice," says Hurter, "was a resolution interwoven, so to speak, with every act of his life."

At the time of his accession to the papal throne the state of the world opened a vast field of activity to the apostolic zeal of Innocent III. The Romans could not yet understand the high destiny which Divine Providence marked out for papal Rome. Civil and political unity were utterly lost political revolutions deluged Sicily with blood; in Lombardy anarchy reigned supreme; in Germany the imperial scepter of Henry VI became an object for strife between three rival claimants; in France, Philip Augustus, blinded by a criminal passion, shocked the world by an incestuous alliance; in England, Richard the Lionhearted fell mortally wounded by an arrow at the siege of Chaluz, leaving the crown to John, his brother, who possessed the qualities neither of a soldier nor even of an honest man; in Spain, the Moors had attained full possession and mastery of all the southern provinces of the peninsula; in the East, the fate of the world was to be irrevocably decided by bloody struggles then raging between Christian civilization and Mohammedan barbarism; while in the West, a sect, more dangerous than Islamism, the Albigensian heresy, under a specious claim of Christian orthodoxy, strove to sap the foundation of all religion, morality and social order. The Church placed this herculean task before the new Pontiff, Innocent III. He was found equal to the work. "If Christianity," says Hurter in the history of this pontificate, "has not been thrown aside as a worthless Creed into some isolated corner of the world; if it has not, like the sects of India, been reduced to a mere theory; if its European vitality has outlived the voluptuous effeminacy of the East, it is due to the watchful severity of the Roman pontiffs, to their unceasing care to maintain the principle of authority in the Church."

From the very beginning of his pontificate, Innocent III had been considering the advisability of launching a new Crusade to win back Palestine, which the powerful arms of Saladin had lately wrested from the grasp of the Christians. A man of his times, Innocent could not fail to be profoundly interested in the Holy Land. He devoted himself throughout his entire pontificate to the cause of the Crusades. He did not cease in spite of one failure after another, to push forward the rescue of the Holy Land from the dominion of the Moslem. The other great object of his pontificate, was the regeneration of both the lay and the clerical elements of the Church. The crowning point of his pontificate was the convocation of an ecumenical council, so that he might lay before the representatives of Europe all that he had done and all that he wished to do. To allow plenty of time for preliminary deliberations, Innocent III issued on April 19, 1213 the bull *Vineam Domini Sabaoth* (The Vineyard of the Lord Sabaoth), calling the spiritual and temporal rulers of the Catholic world to meet together in Rome in November 1215. The result of the summons of the Pope and of the exhortations of his legates was that towards the autumn of 1215 so many people assembled in Rome that "the whole world seemed to be there." There came some 412 bishops, including 71 primates, the Patriarchs of Jerusalem and Constantinople, and representatives of the Patriarchs of Antioch and Alexandria. Also present were more than 800 abbots and priors, and an unknown number of proctors of absent prelates and chapters. In Rome there were bishops from the "Byzantine Empire, the Latin States of Syria, Germany, France, England, Scotland, Ireland, Spain, Portugal, Poland, Hungary, Dalmatia, Sardinia, Corsica, Sicily, Cyprus and Italy." The civil authorities also sent envoys. In a word, there were so many attending the Council that we read of some of them being crushed to death.

Proceedings of the Council

Opening of the Council. Apart from the subsidiary meetings, three formal sessions of the council were held on November 11, 20 and 30, 1215. The council met under the presidency of Innocent III in the Lateran Basilica; hence it was styled the Fourth Council of the Lateran.

The work of the council was threefold: (1) the recovery of the Holy Land; (2) the reform of discipline; (3) the condemnation of the Albigensian heresy.

(1) *The Recovery of the Holy Land.* At the first public session, Innocent himself preached to the assembled multitude, taking for his text: "With desire have I desired to eat this pasch with you before I suffer" (Lk. 22:15), and the Pope added: "Before I die." He first touched upon the state of the Holy Land. In impassioned tones he proclaimed the disgrace which had befallen the name Christian since the Saracens had taken possession of the holy places. He declared that he was at the service of the council, ready, if it saw fit, to go out himself to rouse the Christian nations to free the land which the Redeemer had sanctified by His Blood.

Innocent ordered that on the first of June following, all Crusaders who wished to go by sea to the Holy Land should be at Brindisi ready to embark; those who preferred the land route should set out on the same day accompanied by a papal legate. "In order that nothing may be neglected," said the Pontiff, "in this work of Jesus Christ, we command all the patriarchs, archbishops, bishops, abbots and pastors of souls, to preach seriously the Word of the Cross to those who are confided to their care and to conjure in the name of the Father and the Son and the Holy Ghost all the kings, dukes, princes, marquises, counts, barons and other nobles, the citizens of all cities, towns and villages, that those who themselves cannot depart, will equip a proper number of warriors and furnish them with necessaries for three years; and all this for the remission of their sins. All who will donate ships, or construct them, for this object, will share in the pardon." And that it might not be said that the Pope himself did nothing, Innocent pledged himself to restrict his expenses to the smallest amount, and to donate a ship for the transportation of the Roman contingent. All clergymen were obliged to give to the cause of the Crusades the twentieth part of their revenues for a three-years' period, whereas the cardinals had to give one-tenth.

(2) *Reform of Discipline.* Of the seventy canons issued by the council, some are of lasting importance. Canon 21 reads as follows "Omnis utriusque sexus fidelis, postquam ad annos discretionis pervenerit, omnia sua solus peccata saltem semel in anno fideliter confiteatur proprio sacerdoti, et injunctam sibi poenitentiam pro viribus studeat adimplere, suscipiens reverenter ad minus in Pascha Eucharistiae Sacramentum; alioquin et vivens ab ingressu ecclesiae arceatur et moriens christiana careat sepultura." "All the faithful of both sexes, when they have reached the years of discretion, shall at least once a year confess their sins sincerely to their own priest and shall perform the enjoined penance according to their ability, and receive reverently, at least at Paschal time, the sacrament of the Eucharist, otherwise they shall be debarred from entrance to a church while living, and shall not receive Christian burial when dead." This canon did not institute confession, as unbelievers and antagonists of the Church assert; it simply regulated the time when and how often the sacrament of penance and Holy Eucharist must be received, if one wishes to retain union with the Church. Canon 50 restricts the prohibited degrees of matrimony to the fourth degree of consanguinity. Canon 51 prohibits clandestine marriage, and declares children born thereof illegitimate. The pastor who does not forbid nuptials within the prohibited degrees is suspended from his office for three years.

(3) *Condemnation of the Albigensian heresy.* The errors of the Albigenses, together with the Waldenses, were condemned by this council. The errors may be summed up as follows: There are two Creators, the good God, the author of the invisible world, and the evil God, the author of the visible world. The latter was the author of the Old Testament and was a liar; the former was the author of the New Testament. All the patriarchs, prophets, etc. are damned: John the Baptist was one of the greater demons; the Christ who was born in Bethlehem and

crucified at Jerusalem was also a wicked man. Our souls are apostate spirits of heaven. The sect also denied all the sacraments, infant baptism, Holy Eucharist, etc., matrimony was whoredom, and no one who begot children could be saved. These errors were condemned by the council and the following definition of faith was made by the council: "Firmiter credimus et simpliciter confitemur, quod unus solus est verus Deus, aeternus, immensus, et incommutabilis, incomprehensibilis, omnipotens et ineffabilis, Pater et Filius et Spiritus Sanctus: tres quidem personae, sed una essentia, substantia seu natura simplex omnino... Et unigenitus Dei Filius Jesus Christus, ex Maria semper Virgine Spiritus Sancti cooperatione conceptus, verus homo factus ex anima rationali et humana carne compositus, una in duabus naturis persona, viam vitae manifestjus demonstravit." "We believe firmly and we profess humbly that there is only one true God, immense, and immutable, incomprehensible, almighty and ineffable, the Father and the Son and the Holy Ghost; though three in person, yet one essence, substance or entirely one simple nature... And the only begotten Son of God, Jesus Christ, conceived by the cooperation of the Holy Ghost by the ever Virgin Mary, having become true man, composed of a rational soul and human flesh, one person in two natures, has shown us the way of life rather in a brilliant way."

In stating the doctrine of the Church on the Holy Eucharist against the innovators, this council uses for the first time the term Transubstantiation to express the change that takes place through the words of consecration: "Una vero est fidelium universalis Ecclesia, extra quam nullus salvatur omnino, in qua idem ipse sacerdos est sacrificium Jesus Christus, cujus corpus et sanguis *in sacramento altaris* sub speciebus panis et vini veraciter continentur, *transubstantiatis* pane in corpus et vino in sanguinem potestate divina." "One is the universal Church of the faithful, outside of which no one can be saved, in which the priest himself, Jesus Christ, is the sacrifice, whose body and blood are contained in the *sacrament of the altar* truly under the species of bread and wine, after by divine power bread and wine have been *transubstantiated* into the body and blood."

The errors of the Albigenses and Waldensians were condemned by the council (canons 1 and 3), and because some of their teachings were aimed at the destruction of social life, the Pope ordered a Crusade to be preached against these heretics.

The council also condemned (canon 2) the treatise of Abbot Joachim, which he issued against the Master, Peter Lombard, and in which he advocated a *"Quaternary"* instead of a *"Trinity"* in God.

During this council Innocent III came once more into contact with St. Francis of Assisi, whose sweet, clear voice sounded in winning tones the praises of the simple gospel form of Christian life. Men of all ranks were enraptured and embraced his teaching. The very animals paused in their wantonness to listen to it or laid aside their fierceness to be guided by it. It was a voice that in the midst of the clangor of arms preached peace and, amidst the vagaries of license, proclaimed obedience to authority. The bruised reed it did not break; the smoking flax it did not extinguish. Yet the voice of Francis of Assisi was strong. It forced its way into the hearts of men and women. It was soon the leader of a new and mighty chorus of praise and love that day by day rose up to the throne of God. With his mind full of thoughts of peace and of that respect for authority whence peace flows, Francis' heart naturally turned to him whom he regarded as the earthly representative of the Prince of Peace. He directed his steps toward Rome. There can be no reasonable doubt that Francis was one of the thousands who assembled in Rome for the Lateran Council. Angelo Clareno declares that Innocent III, after the verbal approbation of the Rule of St. Francis in 1209, "in the General Council held in Rome in the year of our Lord 1215 informed all the prelates that he had sanctioned a Rule of Life for St. Francis and those who wish to follow him." From this assertion we may conclude that, though no formal sanction was given by the council to the Rule of St. Francis, the Pope caused it to be regarded by the assembled bishops as one of the already recognized Rules.

Innocent III survived the council till the following year. Although still young when he died, he left an imperishable memory in the history of the Papacy. Sometimes we may like to think of him as Giotti painted him—the youthful Pontiff seated on his modest Gothic throne, his pensive eyes gazing into the distance, while St. Francis of Assisi stands by, expounding that simple life of Christian perfection with which Innocent sympathized so strongly.

XIII
THE THIRTEENTH ECUMENICAL COUNCIL
HELD AT LYONS, FRANCE, IN 1245

WORK OF THE COUNCIL: The excommunication of Frederick II.

There was a close relation between the policy of Innocent III and that of his successor, Honorius III (1266–1227), who was chosen on the morrow of Innocent's death to fill the vacant See. He followed faithfully in his predecessor's footsteps, especially in the matter of the recovery of the Holy Land and of the reform of the Church. Immediately on his elevation to the pontifical throne, Honorius sent a circular letter to the rulers and prelates of the various countries of Europe, exhorting them to a new Crusade, decreed by the Fourth Lateran Council. The Pope and the cardinals contributed a tenth, and all other churchmen a twentieth of their income for three years to subsidize the Crusades.

King Andrew of Hungary was the first to start in answer to the Pontiff's appeal. Soon after a fleet of Northmen and Hollanders came by way of the sea to join the Magyars; but as usual, dissension hindered the full effect of these expeditions. Damietta was taken. St. Francis of Assisi tried to convert the Sultan to Christianity. Not succeeding in his enterprise, he returned to Italy but left some Franciscan friars in the Holy Land for the benefit of pilgrims and for the protection of the holy places. Emperor Frederick II had taken a vow to go on a Crusade and his presence might have made the war a success. Honorius urged him not to delay, but he found one excuse after another to delay, and he postponed his Crusade as many as nine times. He was ready to put off the Crusade for a tenth time, when Gregory IX, who succeeded Honorius III, sent a summons—three days after his consecration—to the Emperor exhorting him to fulfill his vow. After various evidences of bad faith on the part of the Emperor, the Pope excommunicated him. Though under the censure of excommunication, the Emperor now started on a Crusade. He remained in Palestine for nearly two years and negotiated with the Sultan of Egypt. He gained from him a truce of ten years and the restoration of Bethlehem, Nazareth and Jerusalem, except the mosque of Omar. Frederick entered the Church of the Holy Sepulchre in state. As no bishop would crown the excommunicated monarch, he took the crown from the high altar and put it on his head. Frederick returned to Italy, and landing at Brindisi met the Pope at San Germano. Gregory IX made a sincere effort to effect a permanent reconciliation; Frederick promised to restore what he had taken from the Church, to reinstate the banished bishops, and to pay indemnity for the great losses he had caused to the Church. In return for these promises he was absolved from excommunication, but Frederick never meant to do what he had promised. He held such extravagant views of his own boundless power that he was certain to be brought by them into collision both with popular liberty and papal prerogative. He tried to break the power of the Lombard League, and for a time it seemed as if the Papal States and the whole of Italy would fall into his hands. In 1238 Gregory again excommunicated and deposed Frederick.

Gregory died of grief (1241). He was succeeded by Celestine IV, whose pontificate lasted only 17 days. After the See was vacant for a year and a half, due to the machinations of Frederick, Innocent IV was unanimously elected Pope at Anagni (1243). It was hoped that the new Pope would be able to bring about a reconciliation with the Emperor, but the latter's conditions for peace were haughty and unacceptable. When the Pope refused to accept his terms, he marched on Rome and was determined to seize possession of the person of the Pope. Innocent fled to Genoa; thence he betook himself to France where he was received with the greatest reverence and devotion by St. Louis IX, the young King of that realm. On January 3, 1245, Innocent IV sent summons to the bishops to come to an ecumenical council, to be held within six months at Lyons, France. This council is known in history as the First Ecumenical Council of Lyons.

Proceedings of the Council

Opening of the Council. The council was attended by 250 archbishops and bishops, besides many minor prelates, and was presided over by Innocent IV in person. A preliminary session was held in the Monastery of St. Justus, at which 140 bishops were present. This introductory session was held on June 26, 1245.

First Session (June 28, 1245). This session was held in the Cathedral of St. John. After the celebration of Holy Mass, the Pope ascended his throne, and in an eloquent sermon on the text: "According to the multitude of my sorrows in my heart, thy comforts have given joy to my soul" (Ps, xc, 19), he compared his sorrows with the five wounds of our Lord. The first sorrow, he said, was caused by the sins of the higher and lower clergy; the second by the fall of Jerusalem into the hands of the Saracens; the third by the schismatic Greeks who threatened Constantinople; the fourth by the barbarity of the Tartars who had invaded Hungary, murdering all its inhabitants irrespective of age or sex; the fifth by the persecution of the Church by Frederick II. This last point the Pope enlarged upon, enumerating all the serious charges against the Emperor. Frederick was ably, though insolently, defended by his chancellor, Thaddeus of Suessia, whose sophistry failed to impress the assembled bishops, and still less the experienced Pontiff. This ended the first session.

Second Session (July 5, 1245). This session was opened with the same solemnities as the first. A Cistercian bishop of southern Italy preached a vehement sermon against Frederick, to which the imperial chancellor again answered. Thaddeus asked for time to communicate with Frederick. The Pope and the fathers of the council, anxious to make a final effort to effect peace with him, granted a respite of twelve days in which Frederick should make good his justification or advance acceptable propositions. Frederick was unyielding; the hour of justice was at hand.

Third Session (July 17, 1245). The Pope re-enacted a former decree by which the feast of the Nativity of the Blessed Virgin Mary should be kept with an octave. After this, 17 canons—according to others 29 canons—were published, of which the seventeenth Canon is of great importance. It directed the gathering of subsidy for the Crusaders and for the restoration of the Holy Land. After the publication of the canons, Innocent IV proceeded to the excommunication and deposition of Frederick II before the whole council. The prescribed ceremonial for solemn excommunication was carried out. The Pope held a lighted candle in his hand, likewise every bishop. Thaddeus, persisting to the end in his desperate part of imperial advocate, called out aloud: "In the name of my master, Frederick II, I appeal from the sentence you are about to pronounce to the next Pope and to a more General Council." His protest was not heeded. Amid the deep and impressive silence of the august assembly, the Pope read the decree of excommunication directed by the Church against the Emperor: "After mature deliberations with the Cardinals and the Fathers of the Holy Council, We declare Frederick II rejected from the pale of the Catholic Church. We absolve forever from their oath all who have sworn allegiance to him; by the Apostolic authority, We forbid any one henceforth to obey him as Emperor of Germany or King of Sicily, and whoever, hereafter, affords him help and counsel, shall by the very fact incur excommunication. The Electors are bound to name, with as little delay as possible, a successor to rule the empire. As for the Kingdom of Sicily, We shall provide for it, with the advice of our brethren, the Cardinals." At the concluding words of the sentence the Pope and all the bishops extinguished their candles and threw them on the floor. An indescribable emotion seized upon the vast throng which crowded the cathedral. Thaddeus overcome by awe and terror cried aloud "The blow has struck; this is truly the day of wrath and calamity."

Innocent used to the full the rights which medieval Christianity gave him. He could hardly have used them against a more cunning, faithless and withal potent secular ruler than Frederick II.

XIV
THE FOURTEENTH ECUMENICAL COUNCIL
HELD AT LYONS, FRANCE, IN 1274

WORK OF THE COUNCIL: Help for the Holy Land, union of the Greeks with the Latins, reform of morals.

On September 1, 1271, after a three years' vacancy of the Holy See, due to the private ambitions and political discords of the cardinals, the long dissentient voters decided at last to elect to the Chair of Peter, Theobald de Visconti, Archdeacon of Liege, who was at the time apostolic legate in Palestine. This happy outcome was due to the influence of St. Bonaventure. The new Pope received the news of his election at Acre, on October 27, 1271, and took the name of Gregory X (1271–1276). This election revived the drooping spirits of the Christians in the Holy Land. Before leaving Palestine for Europe, the new Pope took leave of the Christians in a most touching address, at the end of which he exclaimed in the words of the Psalmist: "If ever I forget thee, O Jerusalem, let my right hand be forgotten. Let my tongue cleave to the roof of my mouth, if I do not remember thee, if I make not Jerusalem the beginning of my joy" (Ps. 136).

During the whole course of his pontificate, Gregory cherished the project of a new Crusade. His efforts, however, were fruitless and useless amid the general spirit of indifference. Yet this design was the object of his solicitude together with the hope of winning back the Greek Church, which had broken entirely away from the Church of Rome under Michael Cerularius in 1054. This hope of the Pope's heart seemed to be capable of realization in the distant future. The Greek Emperor, Michael Palaeologus, who had again become master of Constantinople, stood in great dread of Charles of Anjou. Whether from motives of policy, or hope to win the mediation of the Pope, or from a sincere desire to bring back his subjects to the bosom of Catholic unity, Michael labored with persevering energy, and succeeded in converting the bishops of his empire to thoughts of union in the face of prejudices from the majority of the Greeks. The Pope sent the Franciscan, John Parastron, to Constantinople; he labored long and faithfully in an effort to bring about a union with Rome, and to acquaint Gregory with the actual and promising conditions. Gregory then despatched four Franciscans—Jerome of Ascoli (later Pope Nicholas IV), Raymond Berengarius, Bonagratia and Bonaventure of Mugello who brought a formula of union to Emperor Palaeologus. These five Franciscans were very active in Constantinople in their effort to bring about the return of the Greeks to the Latin Church.

With a view to adding greater solemnity to the union of the Greek Church with the Latin Church, and to preach a Crusade on a wider scale, the Pope decided to convoke an ecumenical council, to be held in May 1274. Later he selected the city of Lyons in France as the meeting place for the council.

Before setting out for France, Gregory X created St. Bonaventure, General of the Franciscan Order, a cardinal; the same honor was bestowed on the Dominican Peter of Tarantaise (the future Innocent V). After his arrival in Lyons, the Pope sent another request to Emperor Michael Palaeologus to come in person, or to send ambassadors to the council, promising them safe conduct. The Pope also summoned St. Thomas of Aquinas, who set out from Naples in January 1274. St. Thomas never reached Lyons, for he died in the Cistercian Abbey at Fossanuova on March 7, 1274.

Proceedings of the Council

Opening of the Council. After a three days' fast, Gregory X opened the Fourteenth Ecumenical Council in the Cathedral of St. John, Lyons, on Wednesday of Rogation week, May 7, 1274. He committed to St. Bonaventure a great share in the task of guiding the deliberations of the council. According to the best authorities, this council was attended by 13 cardinals, 500 bishops, 70 abbots, and about a thousand minor prelates, in addition to the envoys of the reigning powers, and was presided over by the Pope in person.

First Session (May 7, 1274). Pope Gregory X, after celebrating a Pontifical Mass and after intoning the hymn *Veni Creator* (Come, Holy Ghost) preached the opening sermon in which he laid down the three reasons for holding the council: *help for the Holy Land; union of the Greeks with the Latins;* and *reform of morals.*

Speaking of the needs of the Holy Land, Gregory said: "We have witnessed in person the woes of those generous pilgrims. We have traced, one by one, all their sufferings. Their courage is even greater than their fatigues; their piety is superior to their adversity. Like the warriors of Godfrey de Bouillon, they are worthy sons of the Cross. This is not the time to found new kingdoms in the provinces of Asia. We must march to the rescue of the Holy Sepulchre." At the end of the sermon the first session was closed.

During the interval between the first and second session, the Pope called the archbishops, together with one bishop from each ecclesiastical province, to devise means by which the tithes for the Holy Land could be collected in their respective dioceses. During this time Gregory received very consoling news from his legates in Constantinople concerning the return of the Greeks to the Latin Church, and the Pope immediately communicated the happy news to the council. St. Bonaventure preached on the text: "Arise, O Jerusalem, and stand on high; and look about towards the east, and behold thy children gathered together from the rising to the setting sun" (Baruch, 5:2).

Second Session (May 18, 1274). This session was opened with prayers and ceremonies similar to those which solemnized the first. The Pope preached again on the three objects for which the council was being held. In this session the council formulated the canon on faith, declaring that it is the belief of the Latin and Greek Church that the Holy Ghost proceeds *from the Father and the Son,* from one principle, from all eternity. The Constitution on the procession of the Holy Ghost reads thus: "Fideli ac devota professione fatemur, quod *Spiritus Sanctus aeternaliter ex Patre et Filio,* non tamquam ex duobus principiis, sed tamquam ex uno principio, non duabus spirationibus, sed unica spiratione *procedit*: hoc professa est hactenus, praedicavit et docuit, hoc firmiter tenet, praedicat, profitetur et docet sacrosancta Romana Ecclesia, mater omnium fidelium et magistra: hoc habet orthodoxorum Patrum atque Doctorum, Latinorum pariter et Graecorum incommutabilis et vera sententia. Sed quia nonnulli propter irrefragabilis praemissae veritatis ignorantiam in errores varios sunt prolapsi: Nos hujusmodi erroribus viam praedudere cupientes, sacro approbante Concilio, damnamus et reprobamus, qui negare praesumpserint, aeternaliter Spiritum Sanctum ex Patre et Filio procedere: sive etiam temerario ausu asserere, quod Spiritus Sanctus ex Patre et Filio, tamquam ex duobus principiis, et non tamquam ex uno, procedat." "We profess with a sincere and humble faith that the *Holy Ghost proceeds from all eternity from the Father and the Son,* not as from two principles, but as from one principle, not as from two spirations, but as from one spiration: this the Holy Roman Church, the mother and teacher of all faithful, has so far professed, preached and taught; this she firmly holds, preaches, professes and teaches: this is the immutable and true doctrine of the orthodox Fathers and doctors of the Latins as well as of the Greeks. But because some have fallen into various errors, due to the ignorance of this undeniable truth and wishing to bar the way for these errors, We, with the consent of the Holy Council condemn and reprove those who dare to deny that the Holy Ghost proceeds from the Father and the Son from all eternity, or even assert rashly that the Holy Ghost proceeds as if from two principles, and not as if from one, from the Father and the Son."

Third Session (June 7, 1274). Peter of Tarantaise, Cardinal Bishop of Ostia, preached the sermon. Twelve canons on reform were issued in this session.

The Greek envoys arrived at Lyons on June 24, 1274, and were received with great honors. All the members of the synod went out to meet them and accompanied them to the papal residence, where Gregory X greeted them with marked distinction. They brought letters from the Emperor and from many bishops, and declared they had come to show obedience to the Roman Church. On the feast of Saints Peter and Paul, June 29, 1274, the Pope pontificated in the cathedral in the presence of all cardinals and bishops and the Greek envoys. The Epistle and Gospel were sung in Latin and Greek, and St. Bonaventure preached the sermon. The Credo was sung in Latin and Greek, and the phrase *"Filioque" (and from the Son)* was repeated three times. During the chanting of the Credo, St. Bonaventure stood with the Greeks.

Fourth Session (July 6, 1274). The Cardinal Bishop Peter of Ostia preached. Then the Pope stated again the three reasons for holding the council, and gave expression to his great joy on the return of the Greeks on their own accord to the Roman Church. Thereupon three documents one of the Emperor, the second of the Greek Bishops, the third of the Crown Prince Andronicus were read to the synod. The Emperor repeated the words of the Symbol of Faith, which had been sent to him by Rome, and he declared "I believe in my heart, as I profess with my lips, the true, Catholic, Roman, orthodox faith; I promise ever faithfully to follow it, never to forsake it. I acknowledge the primacy of the Roman Church and the obedience due to it; I pledge myself to all these professions by oath, upon my soul." After this solemn declaration, which after two centuries of struggle and contest put an end to the schism of Photius and Michael Caerularius, Gregory X stood up and intoned the *Te Deum,* while his cheeks were bathed with tears of grateful emotion.

This was the last session in which St. Bonaventure appeared; he died on Sunday, July 15, 1274. The Pope officiated in person at his funeral, to honor by this exception to the pontifical custom the genius and virtue so eminently displayed by the Seraphic Doctor of the Franciscan Order. The Dominican Cardinal Bishop of Ostia, Peter of Tarantaise, preached the funeral sermon on the text: "I grieve for thee, my brother Jonathan" (2 Kings, 1, 26). Many tears flowed, for St. Bonaventure had won the hearts of all who knew him. He exercised the greatest influence over the Greeks whose reunion with the Church he had brought about at the council mainly through his own efforts.

Fifth Session (July 16, 1274). Fourteen canons on reform were issued at this session. Towards its close Gregory X spoke of the great loss which the Church had suffered through the demise of Bonaventure, and he obliged all bishops and priests of the world to offer up one Holy Sacrifice for the repose of his soul. He enjoined that another Holy Mass be offered for all those who had died going to or coming from any council, referring especially to the present one.

Sixth Session (July 17, 1274). Two more canons were issued in this session. The Pope then announced that of the three objects of the council two had been happily settled, namely, the union with the Greeks and the needs of the Holy Land. As for the third, Gregory exhorted all to a better and holier mode of living, adding that, since the council could not remedy all defects at once, he would continue the work which he had begun and provide for the other needs of the Church. Having recited the customary prayers, the Pope imparted the apostolic blessing and dismissed the fathers of the council.

Of the decrees of this council, two claim our particular attention. The *second* canon renewed the decree of Alexander III regarding the election of the Roman Pontiff, and made some additional provisions which experience had shown to be necessary. According to this canon, the cardinals who are in the place where the Pope dies, shall wait only ten days for the arrival of the absent cardinals; then they shall enter upon an election. They should proceed to the Pope's palace, each with only one attendant; or, if necessity demands it in particular cases, with two. In the palace they will be shut up under lock and key (hence the term "Conclave"). No one shall enter or leave the Conclave until after election, and no communication may be had with the outside world, under pain of excommunication. If a Pope is not chosen within three days, only one dish is to be furnished for each cardinal's dinner and supper during the next five days; if the election is not finished on the eighth day, only bread, wine and water will be served until an election is reached. This canon did not please many of the cardinals, and they tried hard, but in vain, to prevent its adoption.

In the *twenty-third* canon the Council promulgated strict regulations against the useless multiplication of religious Orders. "It is not our intention," said the Fathers, "to include the Friars Preachers (Dominicans) nor the Friars Minor (Franciscans) who render such valuable services to the Church. We also approve the Carmelites and Hermits of St. Augustine, whose authorized establishment is anterior to our Decree."

On November 1, 1274 Pope Gregory X published a collection of the 31 decrees of this council which were embodied in the Canon Law.

XV
THE FIFTEENTH ECUMENICAL COUNCIL
HELD AT VIENNE, FRANCE, IN 1311

WORK OF THE COUNCIL: (1) The case of the Knights Templars; (2) help for the Holy Land; (3) reform of morals.

A new period in the history of Church and State began in the latter years of the reign of Philip the Fair, a mockery of the surname—King of France. The stormy years of Boniface VIII, scarcely calmed by the brief reign of Benedict XIII, left the body of cardinals so divided and agitated that the election of a successor was very difficult. The electors met at Perugia; month followed month without any choice being made. Finally, after eleven months, looking outside of their own ranks, the cardinals thought they had secured a suitable candidate for the Papacy in Bertrand de Goth, Archbishop of Bordeaux, a prelate who would be friendly to the French King, and at the same time reverent to the memory of Boniface VIII. Having notified him of his election, they invited him to come to Italy. But he replied by summoning the cardinals to come to France for his coronation. He announced that upon his ascension to the throne, he would assume the name of Clement V (1305–1314).

The removal of the papal residence from Rome to southern France brought about a new condition of things, in which the prestige of the Holy See sank to a lower level. The State became bolder in its encroachments on the domain of the Church; but Divine Providence watching over the Holy See carried it through the storm of the times to new splendor and victories.

Shrinking from the troubles which the Italian factions were stirring up in Rome, Clement V took his abode, first at Lyons, where he was crowned on November 14, 1305, then at Avignon in 1309, a city on the Rhone. Then came the creation of ten new cardinals, all French except one-an Englishman. These new elections changed the composition of the Sacred College. All this helped to dispose the Pope to grant concessions to the insatiable Philip and to the French. First and foremost, the French King called for a condemnation of Boniface VIII. If he had obtained his desire, the great Pontiff would have been tried by a papal court after death, condemned as a heretic, and his body disinterred and burned. But Clement V conscientiously refused to condemn his predecessor. He sought to put off Philip by delay and by granting favors which might placate his hostility. He granted the King the tithes expected from the French dioceses for five years. He modified the bulls of Boniface VIII, declaring that no change in the old relations between the Papacy and the French crown had taken place in any way. Having received all these favors from the Papacy, Philip reiterated his charges and demanded once more that Boniface should be branded as a heretic. Clement finally yielded to his demands so far as to name February 2, 1309, as the time, and Avignon as the place, for a juridical inquiry into the charges brought against Boniface VIII. There was much delay, and after other negotiations, Philip agreed to wait for the coming ecumenical council to have the matter investigated and decided.

Another important matter awaiting the decision of the council was the process against the military order of the Templars. The Knights Templars had their origin in the Crusades and a considerable portion of the glories of the Crusades belongs to them. It had gradually increased in numbers and wealth, until at the time of its suppression it counted 16,000 members and owned extensive properties in nearly all the European countries. The Church had long felt that this increase in worldly possessions had weakened the early spirit of the order and had fostered many abuses among its members. The particular character of the order lent itself to abuses, for it admitted military men whose lives had often been disorderly until their admission, and then professed them without any novitiate, such as other religious orders required. At the same time, the Templars' wealth and privileges made them an object of envy to the mighty. Kings and princes found them formidable and troublesome. Serious charges of unbelief, immorality and insubordination had long been in circulation concerning the members of the order and several popes and synods had censured the Templars. King Philip, having made all his preparations secretly beforehand, arrested all the Templars in France on October 13, 1307, and cast them into prison. Clement V was informed of Philip's encroachment upon ecclesiastical jurisdiction, for the Templars were a religious order depending directly upon the Holy See, and immediately addressed a protest to the King in these words: "You have overstepped the bounds of your authority in constituting yourself the judge of immediate subjects of the Church, and by seizing upon their possessions." Furthermore, to show that he did not limit his protest to mere words, the Pope summoned the entire case of the Templars to be laid before his own tribunal. From this moment on the conduct of Clement V begins to appear in a clear light. The sudden arrest, the trial, the inquiry by torture into their guilt and the capital punishment of the Templars, are the work of Philip, and Philip alone. The juridical inquiry, examination without torture, canonical investigation carefully carried on through four years, and finally the sentence of suppression constitute the part taken by Clement V in this famous trial of the Templars. The Pope's decree, demanding that the whole case be laid before the tribunal, completely disconcerted Philip's plans.

With a view to settling a question which disrupted the world, Clement V in the bull *Alma Mater*, dated April 4, 1310, assigned October 1, 1311 as the opening day of the Fifteenth Ecumenical Council, to be held at Vienne, France.

Proceedings of the Council

Opening of the Council. The council was attended by 20 cardinals, 4 patriarchs, 29 archbishops, of whom one was archbishop-elect, 79 bishops, of whom nine were bishops-elect, and 38 abbots. Clement V presided over it in person. In the bull of convocation the Pope had assigned three reasons for holding the council: (1) The case of the Knights Templars; (2) help for the Holy Land; (3) reform of morals.

First Session (October 16, 1311). This session was opened with great solemnity in the Cathedral of St. Maurice, Vienne. The Pope preached on the text: "In concilio justorum et congregatione magna opera Domini." "In the council of the just, and in the congregation great are the works of the Lord" (Ps. 110, 2, 3). In this sermon the Pope stated the threefold work of the council. After the sermon, two commissions were appointed to examine thoroughly the case of the Knights Templars. Then the Pope dismissed the assembly with his blessing, which he also imparted to the people waiting outside the cathedral.

The council's work concerning the Templars was now taken up in all earnestness. The two commissions consisted of archbishops and bishops, under the Patriarch of Aquileia, who were to examine all the acts relating to the Knights Templars "not perfunctorily, but with precision and plenty of time." In the meantime, the Pope requested the opinions of various cardinals and members of the council in secret sessions. The majority of the commission held that before a juridical condemnation of the whole order was issued, the Templars should be allowed to defend themselves. This decision was rendered early in December 1311. From the end of December to the following February no decision was rendered in the case of the Templars, either by the council or by the Pope. A French delegation arrived in Vienne on February 17, 1312, and for twelve days, until February 29, its members conferred continually with the Pope and five cardinals. Then the ambassadors returned to the King to report the negotiations. On March 2, 1312, the King sent a "humble request" to the Pope to suppress the Templars on account of heresy and many other crimes of which the order was guilty. After the arrival of the King at Vienne on March 19, 1312, secret conferences were held between the Pope and the King. Because the records of these meetings have been either lost or destroyed, we may only surmise the nature of these conferences. The disposition of the temporal possessions of the Templars was most certainly discussed.

On Wednesday of Holy Week, March 22, 1312, Pope Clement assembled all the cardinals and the members of the special commissions in a secret consistory. In their presence, by his supreme authority and without further inquiry, he suppressed the Templars *"by way of provision"* as a matter of policy and discipline.

Second Session (April 3, 1312). Pope Clement V published in this session the bull *Vox in excelso* (A voice from on high) suppressing the Knights Templars in the presence of King Philip and his three sons. Towards the end of the bull of suppression, the Pope declared that he arrived at his decision and sentence after long and mature deliberation and that he disposed of the case in the interests of the Holy Land from the following motives: (1) The order is at least suspected of heresy; (2) the Grand Master and many other members of the order have confessed to the charge of heresy and other crimes and vices; (3) the order has lost its prestige with many bishops and kings; (4) the order, founded in defense of the Holy Land, has lost its usefulness; (5) a delay in the sentence of suppression would entail great temporal losses in the possessions of the order. The Pope added that in the future no one could enter the order, wear its dress, or use the name of Templar under pain of excommunication.

Third Session (May 6, 1312). The Pope published the bull *Ad providam*, to dispose of the property of the Templars. The property of the order was transferred to the Knights Hospitallers of St. John of Jerusalem. The Pope reserved to himself the right to sentence personally the highest dignitaries of the Templars; the others—lesser dignitaries—were left to be dealt with by the provincial councils. He urged clemency in favor of those knights who showed signs of repentance for the crimes which they had confessed. From the property of the suppressed order they were to receive an honorable maintenance. Those who met every charitable admonition of the Church with a stubborn mind were to suffer severe penalties, both civil and canonical.

For many years a heated controversy raged in the Franciscan Order on the right and full meaning and obligation of the vow of poverty, carried on by the spirituals on the one side, and by the community on the other side. Argument followed argument, until the spokesmen for both sides brought the case before the Council of Vienne to receive from it an authoritative pronouncement and decision. Clement V appointed a separate commission of cardinals to examine carefully the interpretation which each party in the dispute gave to the meaning and obligation of poverty. After many meetings held while the council was in progress, Clement V, on May 5, 1312, called the cardinals and representatives of each faction to a secret consistory. In this consistory the controversy was definitely settled. On the following day, May 6, in the third session of the council, Clement V published the Constitution *"Exiti de Paradiso",* which is the official declaration and exposition of the whole Rule of the Franciscan Order, and as such it was incorporated in the acts of the council. Thus the Franciscan Rule is the only Rule approved by an ecumenical council.

In the same session, Clement V published the dogmatic constitution *Fidei Catholicae fundamento* by which some supposed errors of Peter Olivi, a Franciscan Spiritual, were condemned "Dominus papa Clemens in dicta decretali 'Fidei Catholicae fundamento' reprobat tres errores, sc. dicere, quod Christus fuerit vivus lanceatus; item dicere, quod anima rationalis sive intellectiva non sit forma corporis per se et essentialiter; item dicere quod gratia non conferatur parvulis in sacramento baptismi."

The three dogmatic definitions were: (1) The side of Christ was opened *after the death* of the Saviour; (2) the substance of the rational human soul is truly the *form* of the human body; (3) at baptism children and adults alike receive sanctifying grace and the virtues.

The *second object* of the council—*Help for the Holy Land*—was mostly of a pecuniary nature.

Besides issuing the declaration against Philip that Boniface VIII had been a legitimate Pope, thus redeeming the memory of that great Pontiff, the council also promulgated many decrees for the reform of morals. Because a great portion of the acts of this council has been lost, some historians speak of twenty decrees, others of twenty-five decrees. They dealt with ecclesiastical benefices, relations between bishops and princes, the condemnation of the life and practices of the Beghards and Beguines, the monastic discipline and the relation of the mendicant orders to the secular clergy, the election of a Pope, and a variety of other important disciplinary matters. One decree merits the undying gratitude of the literary world; namely, that which introduced the study of Oriental languages in the West. Blessed Raymund Lull, a Franciscan tertiary and martyr, had asked the Holy See repeatedly to establish schools in which the Arabic, Hebrew and Chaldaic languages should be taught in order to prepare missionaries for the conversion of Saracens, Jews and other infidels. At the Council of Vienne he again presented his petition: Petitio Raymundi in concilio generali ad acquirendam Terram Sanctam. The council decreed that Arabic, Hebrew and Chaldaic tongues should be taught publicly wherever the Roman Court was held, as well as in the universities of Paris, Oxford, Salamanca, and Bologna; that two professors should be maintained for each language in the University of Paris by the King of France, and those in the other universities by the Pope and the Bishops.

At the close of the council, the Pope, on the one hand, rewarded those bishops who had attended the council, and, on the other hand, severely reprimanded those who through indifference or negligence had failed to attend.

The Pope intoned the *Te Deum laudamus*. The assembly joined in the singing; the Pope imparted the blessing; the Cardinal Deacon Napoleon sang: "Recedamus in pace" (Let us go in peace) and all Fathers of the Council deeply moved answered: "In nomine Jesu Christi. Amen." (In the name of Jesus Christ. Amen.) And the Master of Ceremonies of the Council adds: "Sic concilium fuit dissolutum." (Thus the Council was dissolved.)

XVI
THE SIXTEENTH ECUMENICAL COUNCIL
HELD AT CONSTANCE IN 1414

WORK OF THE COUNCIL: (1) Removal of the schism; (2) Extirpation of heresy; (3) General reformation of the church "in Head and members."

Toward the end of the fourteenth century a schism, more scandalous even than that of the Greeks, harassed the Church. Pope Clement V, a native of France, was driven by the violence of the Italian nobles to fix his residence at Avignon, in 1309. His successors for the next seventy years followed his example. Italy suffered greatly from the absence of the Popes while Rome, in particular, was torn by contending factions striving for political and civil control. There was a universal and eager cry for the return of the Sovereign Pontiff to his own episcopal See—Rome. At length, in 1377, Gregory XI yielded to the entreaties of St. Catherine of Siena and of the Roman people. He returned to Rome and was welcomed there with great enthusiasm. After his death, the Roman people, fearing that if the new Pope were a Frenchman he would return to Avignon, collected round the building in which the cardinals were assembled for the election and shouted: "We want a Roman Pope." They threatened the Conclave of Cardinals that if their request were not granted, they would make their heads as red as their hats. The terrified cardinals hastily elected the Archbishop of Ban, who took the name of Urban VI (1378–1389). Shortly afterwards they *deliberately confirmed* his election. They were present at the Pope's coronation. Thus they acknowledged him as lawful Pope. Though Urban was remarkable for the piety and austerity of his life, and for his zeal against religious abuses, he was unfortunately a man of stern and inflexible character. His severity soon alienated the love and allegiance of the majority of those who had elected him. All the cardinals, with the exception of four, who were Italians, retired from Rome on various pretexts. They declared their election of Pope Urban null and void because their choice had been made under pressure. They chose another Pope, Cardinal Robert of Geneva, who took the name of Clement VII, and resided at Avignon. This unhappy event threw the Church into confusion, and what is most deplorable, this schism was created by the very men whose sacred duty it was to preserve the Church from such a catastrophe. Christendom was divided by two Popes:

THE POPES DURING THE GREAT WESTERN SCHISM

Lawful Popes	Anti-Popes
Roman Line	*Avignon Line*
Urban VI (1378–1389)	Clement VII (1378–1394)
Boniface IX (1389–1404)	Benedict XIII (1394–1417)
Innocent VII (1404–1406)	
Gregory XII (1406–1415)	

COUNCIL OF PISA'S LINE
Alexander V (1409–1410)
John XXIII (1410–1415)

COUNCIL OF CONSTANCE
Martin V (1417–1431)

Clement VII was recognized in France, Spain, Scotland and Sicily; while Urban was supported and obeyed in England, Germany, Ireland, Hungary, Bohemia and Italy. Excommunications were pronounced by both sides; dissensions increased, and men's minds were troubled by deeds of deplorable violence. The schism was prolonged by the adherents of Clement VII electing a successor on the death of the claimant of the papal throne, who took the name of Benedict XIII. At length, the cardinals and prelates of both factions met in a synod convoked at Pisa in 1409, with the hope of putting an end to the unfortunate schism. They therefore took upon themselves the deposition of Gregory XII, the lawful Pope, and Benedict XIII, the anti-Pope. By the same assumed authority they elected Alexander V as Pope. Their motive was good but their acts were irregular and absolutely wrong. The effect of their acts was the increase of the confusion which already prevailed. Instead of two, there were now three claimants of the Papacy: Gregory XII, Benedict XIII and Alexander V, each of whom was regarded by his own faction as the lawful Pontiff. The jealousy of the cardinals of the several obediences, the conflicting interests of temporal princes, and the animosity of the people seemed to prolong the schism indefinitely. Upon the death of Alexander V, Cardinal Balthasar Cossa was elected Pope, choosing the name of John XXIII. "Of all the miserable consequences of the disastrous Synod of Pisa, this election was the worst." John XXIII was not the moral monster his enemies afterwards endeavored to represent him, but he was utterly worldly-minded and completely engrossed by temporal interests; an astute politician and courtier, not scrupulously conscientious, and more a soldier than a churchman. No help for the distracted Church was to be expected from him. The eyes of the Church, therefore, turned to the powerful and right-minded Sigismund, King of the Romans (1410–1437), who was necessarily deeply interested in the termination of the schism inasmuch as his coronation as Emperor could not take place in Rome until Western Christendom was again united under one spiritual head. He did not disappoint the hopes which were fixed upon him, for the termination of the schism and the restoration of unity in the Church of the West were in great measure his work.

The mischief wrought by the Synod of Pisa did not check the ever increasing belief that peace could only be restored by a general council, but rather increased that belief and brought the question to an issue. A threefold Papacy was a terrible scandal to the Church and made its children long for peace and unity at any price.

The belief that the Emperor, the protector of the Church, was bound to summon a general council became more and more fixed in the public mind. Sigismund understood psychology. He knew how to turn the temper of the time and he also knew how to overcome the great obstacles which stood in the way of the convocation of a general council. Fortune favored him in a remarkable manner. John XXIII was in a precarious condition due to the conquest of Rome by King Ladislaus (June 1413). Sigismund, after he had overcome a prolonged resistance to the idea of the convocation of a council from the cardinal-legates of John, succeeded at length in obtaining their consent to his selection of Constance as the place for the general council. This point settled, Sigismund informed all Christendom that in agreement with John XXIII a general council would be opened at Constance on November 1, 1414. He invited all prelates, bishops, princes, lords and doctors of universities to attend the council. John XXIII, who was completely powerless, had no choice but to submit. On December 9, 1413 he signed the bull which convened a general council at Constance and promised that he would be present. Sigismund wrote also to Gregory XII (the lawful Pope) and to Benedict XIII (the anti-Pope), inviting them to come to the council. The Kings of France and Aragon were also invited to attend.

Proceedings of the Council

Opening of the Council. John XXIII arrived at Constance with nine cardinals on October 28, 1414. He opened the council on November 5, with great splendor. At the time of the strongest representation of the Universal Church at the council, 3 patriarchs, 29 cardinals, 33 archbishops, 150 bishops, over 100 abbots, about 300 doctors of theology and Canon Law, and a great number of inferior clergy, attended.

Three great tasks confronted the council: (1) removal of the schism, which involved the disposal of the three claimants to the Papacy and the election of a universally acknowledged Head of the Church; (2) extirpation of heresy, which under the influence of John Huss was threatening the authority of the Church in Bohemia; (3) general reformation of the Church "in Head and members."

First Session (November 16, 1414). The bull of convocation, issued by John XXIII, was read to the fathers of the council.

The hostility of the party which was most adverse to John XXIII soon manifested itself in the most unmistakable manner. The opposition gained new strength by the arrival of Sigismund on December 24, 1414. Its first great achievement was the new mode of voting by nations, which it introduced for the election of the Pope: French, German, Italian and English. Events unfolded themselves with great rapidity. The prospects of John's party became more and more gloomy. An anonymous memorial, addressed to the fathers of the council and containing most serious charges against John, caused great havoc. His bearing from the beginning of the council had been irresolute, and now he lost heart altogether. On January 22, 1415 Cardinal John Dominici of Ragusa, plenipotentiary of Gregory XII, arrived at the council and publicly declared that Gregory was willing to abdicate his throne unconditionally, if John and Benedict would do the same. Fearing judicial proceedings, John promised to give peace to the Church by his own absolute abdication, but he did not give this promise in good faith.

Second Session (March 2, 1415). John at last came to the conclusion that nothing but bold and strong action could save him. On March 19, 1415, with the connivance of Duke Frederick of Austria, disguised as a messenger, he fled "on a little horse" to Schaffhausen. His flight, motivated by desperation, caused the greatest confusion and alarm among those assembled at Constance.

In this stormy episode of the council, the party which looked for a definite limitation of papal rights as the sole means for suppressing the schism and for reforming the Church gained the upper hand. The general council was ordered and empowered to bring about this limitation of papal power, and accordingly it asserted that the Pope was subject to its jurisdiction. With characteristic precipitation the council decided in its *third* (March 26), *fourth* (March 30) and *fifth* (April 6) *sessions* that a general council could not be dissolved by the Pope without *its* consent; that the present council continued in full force after the flight of John XXIII; that every one, even the Pope, must obey the council in matters of faith, and that an ecumenical council had authority over the Pope just as it had over all Christians.

By these machinations a power, not instituted or delegated by Christ, was conferred upon an assembly—a power which made it superior to the Pope, the Vicar of Christ. These decrees proceeded from a headless assembly. Moreover, the method of its procedure, adopted by a majority of votes, had no precedent in the ancient councils of the Church. The assembly of Constance was no longer an ecumenical council. The great mistake of those assembled was to consider it possible that an ecumenical council could be held without the approbation of the Pope and, in fact, in opposition to him, an opinion as fatal as would be the supposition that a body without a head could be a living organism.

The firmness and prudence of Sigismund had been the chief means of frustrating the attempt made by John XXIII to disperse the assembly. The fate of this Pope was soon decided. In the *sixth session* (April 17) a formula of abdication for John was drawn up; in the *seventh session* (May 2) John was cited before the synod; in the *eighth session* (May 4) the citation of John before the assembly was placarded publicly. In this session the heresies of Wyclif were condemned. John was cited once more in the *ninth session* (May 13). In the *tenth session* (May 14) John was suspended from the government of the Church, and all the faithful were forbidden to obey him. On May 17, John was arrested and confined in Radolfzell. The council had drawn up a list of 72 grievances against John, but in the *eleventh session* (May 23) it reduced these grievances to 54. In the *twelfth session* (May 29) John was solemnly and formally deposed. Utterly broken in spirit, John accepted the sentence of the council and submitted to it without any remonstrance on May 31, 1415. The deposition of John XXIII from the Papacy nullified the work of the Synod of Pisa, and the present Synod of Constance was in an untenable position.

Gregory XII solved the difficulties of the council by his magnanimous resolution to abdicate the throne of Peter. The manner in which this was done is of the highest significance. It must by no means be viewed as a concession in non-essentials to the assembled bishops of the Council. Gregory XII, the one legitimate Pope, sent his plenipotentiary, Malatesta, to Constance, where the cardinals and bishops of his obedience had already assembled. Gregory now lawfully summoned the bishops to the Council—*thirteenth session* on June 15, 1415. Malatesta, acting as his cardinal-legate, read Gregory's bull of convocation to the assembled bishops (*fourteenth session* July 4, 1415), and the bull was unreservedly accepted by all. Malatesta then informed the synod, now lawfully convened, of Gregory's absolute abdication from the throne of Peter. Light had at last broken through the clouds of intrigue and confusion. Gregory's summons had given the synod a legal basis. *It was from now on an ecumenical council.*

"Even if we admit the proposition," observes Phillips, "that Gregory XII's fresh convocation and authorization of the Council were a mere matter of form, this form was the price to which he attached his abdication and it meant nothing less than that the Assembly should formally acknowledge him as the lawful Pope, and accordingly confess that its own authority dated only from that moment, and that all its previous acts in particular those of the fourth and fifth sessions were devoid of all ecumenical character. The recognition of the legitimacy of Gregory XII necessarily included a similar recognition of Innocent VII, Boniface IX and Urban VI, and entailed the rejection of Clement VII and Benedict XIII."

In gratitude for his magnanimous resignation from the Papacy, the council conferred upon Gregory the cardinal bishopric of Porto together with the permanent legation of Ancona, a rank second only to that of the Pope. He did not, however, long enjoy these dignities, as he died a nonagenarian, in the odor of sanctity, on October 18, 1417.

The council now tried to secure the voluntary abdication of Benedict XIII, who was still recognized by Spain, Scotland, Sardinia, Corsica and Minorca. His indomitable and stubborn will gave little hope that he would abandon his pretensions to the Papacy. To obtain the abdication of Benedict, the council appointed in the *sixteenth session,* held on July 11, 1415, a deputation of fourteen legates who should accompany Emperor Sigismund to Benedict for the purpose of obtaining the latter's resignation. In the *seventeenth session,* held on July 14, the council offered prayers for the success of Sigismund's mission. He thereupon departed with his appointed escort. After he had arrived at Perpignan, Sigismund had many interviews with Benedict. The obstinate old man, however, would not consider the matter of resignation, and flatly refused to abdicate. Meanwhile, Ferdinand of Aragon had resolved to withdraw the allegiance of Spain from Benedict. The ambassadors of Castille and Navarre were instructed to do likewise by their sovereigns. Chagrined over the failure of his mission, Sigismund returned to the council. Benedict fled to Peniscola, near Valencia.

During Sigismund's negotiations with Benedict, the council proceeded with its sessions, discussing matter of greater or less importance in the *eighteenth* (August 17), *nineteenth* (September 23), *twentieth* (November 21) and *twenty-first* (February 4, 1416) *sessions*. In the *twenty-second session,* held on October 15, 1416, the Spaniards joined the council and were now reckoned as the fifth nation to be represented there.

In the *twenty-third session* (November 5, 1416), a commission was appointed to examine the charges made against Peter de Luna (Benedict XIII). This commission consisted of twelve members. Twenty-seven grievances were advanced against Benedict, and he was cited several times to appear at the council and submit to its will. The council was occupied with the affair of Benedict from the *twenty-third* to the *thirty-seventh session* (July 26, 1417). The council decided the case by declaring Benedict contumacious, heretical and schismatic, depriving him of all dignity and right, and forbidding the faithful to show obedience to him. Benedict refused to submit. He continued to live as Pope until his death in 1424, surrounded by three cardinals in Peniscola, which he called the "Ark of Noah."

In the *thirty-ninth session* (October 9, 1417), five decrees of reform were published. The first concerned the holding of general councils, which were to be henceforth of more frequent occurrence; the next council was to be held in five years; the following ten years later, and after that every ten years. The second decree enacted measures of precaution to prevent the outbreak of a new schism; the third decree required that every newly-elected Pope make a profession of faith before the proclamation of his election. The remaining decrees limited the transfer of bishops and prelates.

Regarding the election of a new Pope, the council agreed on October 28, 1417, that thirty other prelates and doctors—six for each nation—should be associated with the cardinals present at Constance. This decree, as well as the other decree for securing reform, was immediately published in the *fortieth session* (October 30, 1417). The decree on reform commanded that before the dissolution of the council the new Pope should take measures for ecclesiastical reform, especially in reference to the Supreme Head of the Church and the Roman Court. He should effect this reform either with the co-operation of the members of the council or with the deputies of the nations.

The Conclave began in the *forty-first session* on November 8, 1417, in the Merchants' Hall at Constance with fifty-three electors, of whom twenty-three were cardinals, and thirty deputies of the nations, present on the feast of St. Martin, November 11, 1417. The Cardinal Deacon, Otho Colonna, came forth from the council as Pope Martin V.

There was indeed cause for the unbounded rejoicings of the Catholic world, for the unity of the Church was restored. These evidences of joy re-echo through the pages of the histories written by the ancient chroniclers of this period. "Men could scarcely speak for joy," says one of the historians. The Church had again a Head—the great and deplorable Western schism was at an end. These nine and thirty years of division caused by the cardinals were the most terrible crisis through which the Roman Church had passed in all the centuries of her existence. An uncompromising opponent of the Papacy has acknowledged that any secular kingdom would have perished in such a crisis; yet so marvelous was the organization of this spiritual dynasty, and so indestructible the idea of the Papacy, that the schism only served to demonstrate its indivisibility.

In the *forty-second session* on December 28, 1417, Martin V treated of the release of Balthasar Cossa (John XXIII), and of the elevation of the Bishop of Winchester to the cardinalate.

In the *forty-third session* on March 21, 1418, seven decrees on reform were published, and treaties which were entered into with Germany, France and England were accepted by the council.

In the *forty-fourth session* on April 19, 1418, Pope Martin V announced the time and place of the next council—to be held in 1423 at Pavia.

In the *forty-fifth session* on April 22, 1418, Pope Martin declared the Council of Constance closed. The council had accomplished the first task placed before it, namely, the removal of the schism by the election of Martin V as the one universally acknowledged Head of the Church.

The *second task*—that of extirpation of heresy—the council accomplished by condemning the heresies of John Wyclif of England and of John Huss of Bohemia. The deplorable Western Schism offered Wyclif the opportunity he desired and which he used under the guise of zeal for the Church—the opportunity to calumniate the Holy See. His ill-feeling toward Rome soon developed into open opposition to the Church in general. Without any knowledge of Greek and Hebrew, he began in 1380 to translate the Bible into English, omitting from his work the deutero-canonical books. He declared the Bible the only source of faith and denied the doctrine of the freedom of the will and the dogma of Transubstantiation. Further, he defended the doctrine of unqualified predestination and taught that the Papacy and Episcopacy are not of divine institution. He went so far as to teach that all power, spiritual as well as temporal, is dependent on the state of grace and that the Church is only the communion of the predestined. A synod, held in London in May 1382, had condemned 24 articles, drawn from the writings of Wyclif, and the Council of Constance condemned 45 propositions taken from the books of the same heretic.

John Huss, an ardent defender of the errors of Wyclif, promulgated in his preaching Wyclif's heretical doctrine in Bohemia, and while doing so he made the most odious attacks on the clergy. The errors of Huss are almost identical with those of Wyclif, except that Huss did not accept the Wyclifist doctrine on the Holy Eucharist. John Huss denied that the priest had the power to absolve from sin, conceding to him only the right of declaring that God had forgiven the penitent's sin. Having been commanded by his Archbishop Sbinko to burn his heretical writings, Huss raised a storm of protest. This brought upon him the excommunication of John XXIII, who at the same time enunciated the penalty of interdict on Prague as long as Huss should remain there. Sigismund cited John Huss to appear before the Council of Constance to defend himself. He set out for Constance protected by a letter of safe-conduct from King Sigismund. At first, the council treated the heretic with mildness. After a long preliminary examination, the public trial of Huss took place on June 5th, 7th and 8th, 1415. The council rejected the heretical teachings of Huss, who refused to revoke them. Because of his refusal he was degraded from his sacerdotal dignity on July 6th, and handed over to the secular power for punishment. Huss remained obstinate to the end; he declared the Council of Constance to be an assembly of Pharisees. He was burned at the stake on July 6, 1415. His friend and follower, Jerome of Prague, suffered the same fate on May 30, 1416.

The *third* purpose for which the Council had been summoned was the reformation of the Church "in Head and members." Through all the deliberations on reform, the nations could agree neither on the points proposed by the reform commission nor on the amendments proposed by the Pope. Thus, the movement for a reform ended in a compromise. The council, as a whole, accepted seven decrees. Concerning the other points, Martin V concluded separate concordats with the German and Latin nations for five years, and with the English nation in the form of a permanent charter.

Sigismund made every effort to induce Pope Martin V to take up his residence in Germany; Basel, Strassburg, Mayence were offered to him as places of abode. The French begged him to reside at Avignon, as so many of his predecessors had done. But Martin V was not willing to become dependent on any foreign power, and hence he firmly declined all these proposals. In the absence of its chief Pastor, the inheritance of the Church was, he said, destroyed and despoiled by tyrants. In order to prevent its complete destruction, he must go, hence he begged them to let him depart. Since the Roman Church is the Head and Mother of all churches, in Rome alone is the Pope at his post, like the pilot at the helm of his vessel. The conditions of the States of the Church undoubtedly demanded the return of the Pope, and Martin V acted prudently in resolving to return to Italy and to Rome. He left Constance on Pentecost Monday, May 16, 1418. Amidst the rejoicings of the people he travelled through Berne to Geneva. From Geneva the Pope went to Mantua; there he remained from October 1418 to February 1419. The critical conditions of the States of the Church compelled him to spend nearly two years in Florence, until he finally made his solemn entrance into the Eternal City on September 30, 1420, where he was enthusiastically welcomed by the people of Rome as their deliverer.

XVII
THE SEVENTEENTH ECUMENICAL COUNCIL
HELD AT BASEL, FERRARA, FLORENCE FROM 1431 TO 1442.

WORK OF THE COUNCIL: (1) Extirpation of heresy and of the Greek Schism; (2) re-establishment of peace among Christian Princes; (3) reform of the Church "in Head and members."

According to the decision of the Council of Constance, general councils were henceforth to be held at appointed periods. The extraordinary remedy which had hitherto been employed only in desperate crises and at rare intervals, and which proved to be beneficial only in certain circumstances, was made a common and ordinary remedy. Instead of once in a century, or, at most, once in fifty years, a council was now to be convoked every five or ten years. The aim of this innovation was to substitute constitutional for monarchial government in the Church.

Martin V was absolutely opposed to any attempt to alter the constitution of the Church. From his point of view he was no doubt perfectly right. Erroneous ideas regarding the constitution and position of a council were at this time widely diffused, threatening the very foundation of papal power, and it was the Pope's duty to consider how they might be set right. The endless disputes as to whether the Pope or the council was to hold the first place in the Church, and the pretensions of the Synod of Pisa and the Council of Constance (4th and 5th sessions) to dictate to the Pope, had not only filled Martin V with distrust but inspired in him a real horror of the very name of a council. He could not, however, venture to oppose the movement openly. Accordingly, he summoned a council to meet at Pavia in 1423. Circumstances were most unfavorable for such an assembly. England and France were engaged in a bloody conflict; Germany was laid waste by the Hussites, and war with the Moors was raging in Spain. It was evident that the council which opened at Pavia on April 23, 1423, could not be adequately attended. In June the council had to be transferred to Siena because a plague broke out in Pavia. Now in Siena it soon became plain that the attitude of the council towards the Pope was identical with that of the Council of Constance. Matters were made worse by the hostile position assumed by King Alfonso of Aragon, who endeavored to incite the fathers of the council against the Pope. Martin V accordingly made the small attendance of prelates and their dissensions a pretext for suddenly dissolving the council on February 26, 1424. All archbishops, bishops and others were strictly forbidden to attempt its continuation. Before the publication of the decree of dissolution, Basel had been selected as the place for a new council, and it was scheduled to meet in seven years.

On January 1, 1431, Martin V appointed Cardinal Cesarini to act as legate of the Apostolic See for the forthcoming crusade against the Hussites. A month later the Pope decided that Cesarini should preside over the Council at Basel—from its beginning and should undertake its guidance. The aim of the council was to be: (1) the extirpation of heresy and of the Greek Schism; (2) the re-establishment of peace among Christian princes; (3) the reformation of the Church "in Head and members." Two papal bulls were prepared for Cesarini; the first authorized him to open the council and preside over it; the second, in case of necessity, empowered him to dissolve it or to transfer it to another city. The latter bull clearly indicated the attitude which Martin V intended to assume towards the council. He justly apprehended that the council would attempt further encroachments on the papal authority, which had already been seriously impaired by the Western Schism, but before the necessity for extreme measures had arisen, Martin V died of apoplexy on February 20, 1431. He was succeeded by Eugene IV (1431–1447), a nephew of Gregory XII.

Cardinal Cesarini was engaged in launching the crusade against the Hussites when he received the appointment as President of the Council of Basel. It was not till September 9, 1431, that he arrived at Basel. The attendance at the council was very poor in the beginning. A report of this fact was sent to Eugene IV, who, due to misrepresentations issued a bull, December 18, 1431, dissolving the council and transferring it to Bologna, to be opened in that city after the lapse of eighteen months.

Proceedings of the Council

Opening of the Council. On December 14, 1431, Cardinal Cesarini, in the presence of three bishops, fourteen abbots and a great number of doctors of universities solemnly opened the council. When the bull of dissolution arrived in Basel, those assembled evaded the issue of reading publicly the bull on January 13, 1432, by absenting themselves from the place of meeting. Cardinal Cesarini urged the Pope to recall the bull of dissolution. Unfortunately, his efforts were in vain; Eugene would not yield. Cesarini resigned as president of the council. In order to defend themselves against the Pope, the members of the synod proceeded to re-assert the revolutionary resolutions by which the Council of Constance declared itself superior to the Pope.

Second Session (February 15, 1432). Measures more hostile to the power of the Papacy soon followed. In the *third session* held on April 29, 1432, the Pope and his cardinals were formally summoned to Basel. The council threatened to institute proceedings against them for contumacy in event of their failure to appear before the council within a period of three months. An order, published on September 26, 1432, admitted representatives of the lower ranks of the clergy to the council in such overwhelming numbers, that the higher ecclesiastics were completely deprived of the moderating influence so necessary in such assemblies.

It is impossible to justify the course taken by the Synod of Basel. It soon overstepped all bounds in its opposition to Eugene IV. The danger which threatened the Papacy and the Church was of incalculable magnitude for if the Basel resolutions were carried into effect the overthrow of the divinely established constitution of the Church was inevitable, and the Vicar of Christ would become merely the first official of a constitutional assembly. If priests dealt in a similar manner with their bishops, and the faithful with their priests, the dissolution of the whole Church would be the inevitable consequence. The synod had entered upon a course which was leading unmistakably and inevitably to a new schism, and this was clearly perceived in Rome.

At last the gravity of the whole situation induced Eugene IV to yield and to enter into negotiations with the council. The Pope recalled the decree of dissolution in 1431; acknowledged the council as ecumenical in its origin by a bull of December 15, 1433, demanding, however, that his legates preside at the council, and that all acts of the council against his person and against the authority of the Apostolic See should be revoked.

The reconciliation of the council with the Pope had only the semblance of sincerity, and the feelings of the majority remained unchanged, so that the fanatical partisans of the council soon gained the upper hand in the assembly. Their leader was the French Cardinal Louis D'Allemand of Aries, and their object was to make the council a permanent corporation and institution and to endow it with all the attributes of sovereignty, admitting the Pope as its more or less necessary appendage. Instead of the reform of ecclesiastical abuses, the decreasing of the papal authority became the chief business of the synod.

From the very beginning of the council the Hussites had been invited to attend. In January 1433, Procopius, leading a band of four hundred Hussites, arrived at Basel and made the following demands: (1) Communion *under both species* for the laity; (2) the right to preach the Word of God for all priests without restriction of place; (3) the promulgation of canonical regulations forbidding ecclesiastics to hold temporal possessions; (4) the declaration that every one of the faithful be authorized to punish public sinners with his own hand and according to his own judgment. The council rejected these demands, and the deputies of the Hussites left Basel. However, they resumed conferences in Bohemia with this final result: (1) the Bohemians may receive Holy Communion under both species, but the priests must always explain that the Body and Blood of Christ were equally and fully present under each species of the Eucharist; (2) every priest possesses the right to preach the Gospel but he must always remain subject to the approval of the bishop; (3) ecclesiastics have the right to hold temporal possessions—this grant is warranted by examples found in both the Old and the New Testament—but the Church has the power and the will to prevent or to reform abuses by wise regulations; (4) the right to punish public crimes belongs directly, in spiritual matters, to the ecclesiastical tribunals; in temporal concerns, to the civil magistrates. Any canonical decree to the contrary would only make vengeance lawful, perpetuate feuds, and authorize countless murders. Upon the basis of these grants, a concordat was drawn up by the Church to the satisfaction of the moderate Hussites. The Council of Basel sanctioned these grants of rights and privileges. In this matter the conduct of the Council of Basel was irreproachable, but soon other decrees were formulated, which were directed against the authority of the Pope.

The new proceedings were so prejudicial to the undoubted rights of the Holy See that Eugene IV was constrained to address a memorial to all the European powers, making bitter complaints of the unheard-of presumption of the synod. The council had, he says, degraded his legates by arbitrarily limiting their authority; by making their presidency merely nominal by publishing its decisions without their consent; transformed itself into a headless body; subjected the Pope, by a false interpretation of the decrees of the Council of Constance, to the censorship of the synod in a manner unknown in former times; granted papal dispensations; demanded for itself revenues which were refused to the Pope; assumed the right to deal with cases reserved to the Holy See, and suppressed the prayer for the Pope in the liturgy. For these and many other reasons the Pope deemed that it was time for the princes to recall their bishops and ambassadors from Basel, and thus render possible the assembling of another and better-disposed council.

The complaints of Eugene, who was unwilling to let his high dignity become a mere shadow, were fully justified, for the conduct of the clerical democracy at Basel went beyond all bounds. The majority of the assembly consisted of Frenchmen, who offered no opposition to any measure directed against the Pope. The most fanatical party seized every opportunity of making the Pope feel their power and ill-will. Their real aim the Bishop of Tours declared with admirable candor in one of the sessions in the following words: "We must either wrest the Apostolic See from the hands of the Italians, or else despoil it to such a degree that it will not matter where it abides." The council would have proceeded yet further in its destruction of papal dignity and power but for a crisis precipitated by the negotiations of the Greek Church for union with the Latin Church.

The history of these negotiations shows that Eugene IV, alone, sought sincerely for this union. The Greek Emperor used the idea of a union with Rome as a talisman to procure the aid of the West against the Turks. The members of the Council of Basel hoped by utilizing the insincerity of the Emperor to gain a fresh victory over the Pope. The choice of the place where the union council should meet led to fresh discord between the Pope and the assembly at Basic. In the *twenty-fifth session* held on May 7, 1437, the council arrived at an important decision. The anti-papal party, led by Cardinal D'Allemand, had shortly before this session so strengthened itself by the admission of a number of ecclesiastics from the neighborhood of Basic that it could command a majority of the votes of the council. Amidst violent opposition it decided that Basel should be the place of meeting, or, if this city were not convenient for the Greeks, that Avignon would be selected, or some other city in Savoy; also that a general tithe should be levied on Church property to meet the necessary expenses of the council. A minority of the assembly, headed by Cardinal Cesarini, voted for the selection of Florence or Udine as the city for the council because those places had been proposed by the Pope.

The Pope approved of the decision of the minority. He did everything in his power to hinder the carrying out of the decree of the majority. He saw plainly the object of the projected and contemplated transfer of the council to Avignon. This would mean after his death or deposition the establishment of the Roman Court under French protection in the latter city. This explains the obstinacy with which Cardinal D'Allemand and his followers held to the plan of selecting Avignon in spite of the objections of the Pope, who vividly remembered the disastrous results of the sojourn of his predecessors in that city. The objections of the Greeks to the selection of Avignon as the place for the council frustrated all negotiations between them and the party of Cardinal D'Allemand, while the superior skill of the papal diplomatists completely won the Greeks over to the side of Eugene IV.

The Pope's success provoked his adversaries at Basel to the utmost, and on July 3, 1437 they issued a decree in which, after pouring forth a torrent of accusations against him, they summoned him to appear before their tribunal. The Pope replied to this summons by a bull, published on September 18, 1437, in which he declared that the six years' duration of the Council of Basel had produced surprisingly small results; and he made known to all Christendom its evil doings. Upon the publication of this bull, the synod was to discontinue its work at once, except in regard to the Hussite affair hence to complete its work the council might continue for thirty-one days more. Should the members of the synod continue their outrageous activity, the Council of Basel would be automatically concluded and transferred to Ferrara, a city more convenient for the Greeks.

The synod declared the Pope's bull invalid and threatened him with suspension and deposition. In vain did Cardinal Cesarini endeavor again to make peace. In a long discourse he earnestly entreated the members of the synod to lay aside all hatred and strife, but his words fell upon deaf ears. Cesarini with his numerous friends then left Basel for Ferrara.

The members of the Synod of Basel stubbornly continued their work; they went even so far as to elect an anti-Pope in the person of Duke Amadeus of Savoy, who took the name of Felix V. The synod, however, came to an inglorious end in 1449.

The Council of Basel—only in those sessions and in those measures which were recognized by the Pope and the Council held at Ferrara-Florence, which Pope Eugene IV summoned as the continuation of the Council of Basel, form together the Seventeenth Ecumenical Council. Therefore the first twenty-five sessions of the Council of Basel must be distinguished from the rest. The latter sessions are obviously schismatic, and even of the former sessions only those decrees are to be regarded as ecumenical which treat of the extirpation of heresy, of the maintenance of peace in Christendom, and of the reformation of the Church, provided these decrees contained nothing in them which lessened or detracted from the authority and dignity of the Apostolic See.

At the opening of the Council of Constance (1414), a delegation, consisting of twenty-one persons, sent by the Greek Emperor and the Patriarch of

Constantinople, arrived for the purpose of bringing about a union between the Greek and Latin Church. But the project did not materialize because the delegates lacked full powers to subscribe to a union. Joseph, Archbishop of Ephesus, became Patriarch of Constantinople on May 21, 1416. He sent John Eudaemon with new proposals to the Council of Constance and entered into negotiations with the newly-elected Martin V. Letters were exchanged between the Pope and the Patriarch—both prelates asked for a union council. Martin V sent Anthony Messanus, a Franciscan, to Constantinople to submit nine proposals to the Oriental Church on the basis of which a union might be brought about. Because the conditions advanced by the Emperor of the East were well-nigh impossible to fulfill, negotiations between the East and the West were broken off.

In 1430 the Mahometans captured Saloniki; thus imminent danger threatened Constantinople. To solicit help from the West, under the pretext of religion and union, an embassy was sent from Constantinople to Rome. Eugene IV, who had succeeded Martin V, considered it an important task of his pontificate to bring about the union with the Greeks. The embassy arrived in Rome about the same time that word was received from Basel that the council then in session was poorly attended. This fact, and the request of the Greeks to hold a union council in an Italian city, determined Eugene to dissolve the Council at Basel (1431) and to transfer it to Bologna in Italy where it should convene in eighteen months. This act of the Pope caused great dissension between the council and himself. The Baseleans tried hard to win the Greeks over to their side. But the Greeks espoused the cause of the Pope, and when all negotiations were finished they embarked for Italy on November 24, 1437 on a fleet furnished by the Pope, who also defrayed all their expenses during the council.

After a perilous voyage, the Greeks landed in Venice on February 8, 1438. There they were received with great honors. Having been informed that the Pope had selected Ferrara as the place for the *Union Council,* the Greeks left Venice on February 28, and arrived at Ferrara on March 4.

Cardinal Albergati had opened the council on January 8, 1438, at the behest of Pope Eugene IV. In the *first session* on January 10, 1438, the Synod of Basel was excommunicated. On January 24, Pope Eugene arrived at Ferrara. On February 15 the *second session* was held under the presidency of the Pope, at which seventy-two bishops were present. The council declared the decrees of Basel null and void, and pronounced excommunication and deposition on the obstinate prelates, who persisted in carrying on the council despite the papal bull of dissolution.

On March 4, 1438, Emperor John Palaeologus, accompanied by twenty-two archbishops and bishops and eleven abbots, also by a large number of Greek senators and nobles—in all seven hundred persons—arrived at Ferrara for the purpose of accomplishing the long-talked-of and much-desired reconciliation of the Greek schismatics with the Roman See. Joseph, Patriarch of Constantinople, an ardent advocate of the union, arrived at the council on March 7, and all were received with great enthusiasm.

The Union Council at Ferrara

The Union Council was formally opened on April 9, 1438. Due to sickness the Patriarch Joseph was unable to attend. Everything seemed ready for the consummation of the great object of the council when the Greek Emperor requested that the Western sovereigns should be present at the reunion either in person or through their envoys. Seven months of delay ensued before the Latins and Greeks could again meet in full council. Meanwhile, however, they held many conferences, in which there were discussions on the doctrines of the procession of the Holy Ghost from the Father and the Son, on purgatory, and on the Beatific Vision, on the use of leavened or unleavened bread in Holy Eucharist, and on the supremacy of the Roman Pontiff. Most of these conferences were held in the Franciscan church and were conducted by a Latin and Greek commission, each consisting of ten members. While these conferences were in progress, the Greeks obstinately refused to discuss the doctrine of the procession of the Holy Ghost, but they agreed to consider the doctrine on purgatory and the Beatific Vision. After they had heard the exposition of the belief of the Roman Church on these latter points, they declared that Rome's faith differed little from their teaching. The Greeks admitted the existence of a middle state, in which souls after death not entirely purified from the stains of sin are temporarily detained, and that these souls are relieved by the prayers and sacrifices of the Church Militant, but they excluded from this state of purgation the pain of fire, which they regarded as peculiar to the hell of the damned; and even in hell only after the General Judgment. The conferences soon degenerated into theological altercations, and it seemed as if the work of the council would come to naught. After a while things took a better turn, and the *First Session of the Union Council* (the *third* since its beginning in Ferrara) was held on October 8, 1438. Six prominent members were chosen from each side to discuss the great questions at issue. The Latins selected Cardinal Cesarini; Andrew, Archbishop of Rhodus; Louis, Bishop of Forli; Peter Perquiere, a Franciscan, and the two Dominicans John of Montenegro and John Torquemada. The Greeks chose Bessarion, Archbishop of Nicaea; Mark, Archbishop of Ephesus, an obstinate opponent of the union; Isidore, Archbishop of Kiev; and three others. In the first session, Bessarion, out of deference to the Greeks, was given the privilege of addressing the council.

Second Session (October 11, 1438). Archbishop Andrew of Rhodus spoke on the union in glowing words.

Third Session (October 14, 1438). Archbishop Mark of Ephesus assailed the Latin Church vehemently on account of the addition of *"Filioque" ("and from the Son")* to the Creed, and demanded the suppression of this addition in the Creed. Cardinal Cesarini answered: "If the addition is blasphemous, prove it and suppress it if it is correct, receive it!" The Greeks were now forced to enter on an examination of the doctrine of the Procession. In vain the Emperor besought the Pontiff to have the discussions take place in private sessions. The dogma of the procession of the Holy Ghost from the Father *and the Son* occupied the attention of the council from the *fourth* to the *fifteenth session* (October 1, 16, 20, 25, November 1, 4, 8, 11, 15, December 4, 8, 1438).

The plague broke out in Ferrara towards the end of the year 1438, and desolated the city; many Greek members of the council fell victims to the pestilence. In addition to this, the horrors of war were approaching Ferrara.

In the *sixteenth session*, held in January 1439, Pope Eugene IV decreed that the council should be transferred from Ferrara to Florence. The Greeks were averse to the transfer, but the Pope declared that he could no longer pay them the promised subsidies as he had at Ferrara, and that he had been obliged to accept a loan from Cosmo of Medici on condition that the council be transferred to Florence. If the Greeks would agree to the transfer, the Pope promised to furnish money and two galleys for the defence of Constantinople; to satisfy all the wants of the visitors, and to allow them, united or schismatic, to depart in three or four months. Cosmo of Medici received the members of the council with a magnificence which befitted the chief magistrate of Florence and the wealthiest individual in Europe.

The Union Council at Florence

Seventeenth Session (February 26, 1439). Cardinal Cesarini and the Emperor discussed the subjects to be treated in future sessions.

Eighteenth Session (March 2, 1439). The first public disputation on the procession of the Holy Ghost took place between the Dominican Provincial of Lombardy, John of Montenegro, and Mark, Archbishop of Ephesus. These disputations continued for the next *five sessions* (from the 19th to the 23rd Session).

The *twenty-fourth* and *twenty-fifth sessions* were held respectively on March 21 and 24, 1439. Archbishop Mark of Ephesus and Archbishop Anthony of Heraclea deliberately absented themselves from the sessions. The Greeks were divided into two parties. The one which favored a union was headed by Bessarion and Isidore. The other, which was directly opposed to the union, was headed by Mark of Ephesus. Bessarion delivered a magnificent speech before the Greeks on April 13th and 14th, urging that the union between the Greeks and Latins be accomplished. The result was the selection of ten men who should devise a formula of union.

On June 8, 1439, a deputation of the Greeks waited upon Eugene IV and declared: "We agree with you that the addition to the Creed as you recite it, is derived from the Holy Fathers; we approve it and we are united with you; we declare that the Holy Ghost proceeds from the Father *and the Son,* as from *one Principle and Cause.*" The Greeks were not forced to insert the addition *"and from the Son"* into their Creed as long as they accepted the dogma.

On June 9, Pope Eugene demanded a settlement of the other important questions concerning the use of unleavened or leavened bread, the Beatific Vision and purgatory, and the primacy of the Pope.

THE SEVENTEENTH ECUMENICAL COUNCIL 81

On July 6, 1439, Pope Eugene IV, all the members of the council and the Emperor assembled in the cathedral. Cardinal Cesarini ascended the pulpit, and read in Latin the Apostolic Constitution: *Laetentur caeli* (Let the heavens rejoice); it was the dogmatic definition of the Union Council "In nomine Sanctae Trinitatis, Patris et Filii et Spiritus Sancti, hoc sacro universali approbante *Florentino* Concilio definimus, ut haec fidei veritas ab omnibus Christianis credatur et suscipiatur, sicque omnes profiteantur, quod Spiritus Sanctus ex Patre et Filio aeternaliter est et essentiam suam suumque esse subsistens habet ex Patre simul et Filio, et ex *utroque aeternaliter* tamquam *ab uno principio et unica spiratione procedit;* declarantes, quod id, quod sancti Doctores et Patres dicunt, ex Patre per Filium procedere Spiritum Sanctum, ad hanc intelligentiam tendit, ut per hoc significetur, Filium quoque esse secundum Graecos quidem causam, secundum Latinos vero principium subsistentiae Spiritus Sancti, sicut et Patrem. Et quoniam omnia, quae Patris sunt, Pater ipse unigenito Filio suo gignendo dedit, praeter esse Patrem, hoc ipsum quod Spiritus Sanctus procedit ex Filio, ipse Filius a Patre aeternaliter habet, a quo etiam aeternaliter genitus est. Definimus insuper, explicationem verborum illorum *'Filioque'* veritatis declarandae gratia, et imminente tunc necessitate, licite ac rationabiliter Symbolo fuisse appositum.

"Item, in *azymo* sive *fermentato* pane triticeo corpus Christi veraciter confici; sacerdotesque in altero ipsum Domini corpus conficere debere, unumquemque scilicet juxta suae Ecclesiae sive occidentalis, sive orientalis consuetudinem.

"*(De novissimis).* Item, si vere poenitentes in Dei cantate decesserint, antequam dignis poenitentiae fructibus de commissis satisfecerint et omissis, eorum animas poenis purgatoriis post mortem purgari: et ut a poenis hujusmodi releventur, prodesse eis fidelium vivorum suffragia, Missarum scilicet sacrificia, orationes et eleemosynas, et alia pietatis officia, quae a fidelibus pro aliis fidelibus fieri consueverunt secundum Ecclesiae instituta. Illorumque animas, qui post baptisma susceptum nullam omnino peccati maculam incurrerunt, illas etiam qui post contractam peccati maculam, vel in suis corporibus, vel eisdem exutae corporibus, prout superius dictum est, sunt purgatae, in caelum mox recipi et intueri dare ipsum Deum trinum et unum, sicuti est, pro meritorum tamen diversitate alium alio perfectius. Illorum autem animas, qui in actuali mortali peccato vel solo originali decedunt, mox in infernum descendere, poenis tamen dispanibus puniendas.

"Item definimus, sanctam Apostolicam Sedem, et Romanum Pontificem, in universum orbem tenere primatum, et ipsum Pontificem Romanum successorem esse beati PETRO principis Apostolorum et verum Christi vicarium, totiusque Ecclesiae caput et omnium Christianorum patrem ac doctorem exsistere; vel ipsi in beato pascendi, regendi ac gubernandi universalem Ecclesiam a Domino nostro Jesu Christo plenam potestatem traditam esse; quemadmodum etiam in gestis oecumenicorum Conciliorum et in sacris canonibus continetur."

This dogmatic definition of the Union Council declares: that the Holy Ghost proceeds from the Father *and the Son;* that leavened or unleavened bread are equally valid matter of the Holy Eucharist, but commanded that each priest must follow the custom of his church; that the just, dying before their sins are entirely expiated, are purified in purgatory, and are there assisted by the sacrifices, prayers and alms of the faithful; that the completely purified soul is received into heaven there to enjoy the Beatific Vision of the triune God according to their merits; that those who die in actual mortal sin, descend into hell, there to undergo punishment; that the Roman Pontiff is the successor of Blessed Peter, Prince of the Apostles; that he is the true Vicar of Jesus Christ, the head of the Universal Church, and the father and teacher of all Christians; that Christ has given to him, in the person of Blessed Peter, the full power of teaching and governing the Universal Church.

After Cesarini delivered the dogmatic definitions of the Church, Bessarion mounted the pulpit and read the Greek version of the definition of faith. This definition was signed *for the Greeks:* by the Emperor, four representatives of the Greek patriarchs, sixteen archbishops, four deacons and the envoys of some other Greek princes. Mark of Ephesus stubbornly refused to sign the definition. The definition was signed *for the Latins:* by the Pope, eight cardinals, two latin patriarchs, sixty-one archbishops and bishops, forty abbots, four generals of religious orders, and the envoys of the Duke of Burgundy.

The original document is still preserved in the Laurentiana Library in the city of Florence.

Towards the end of July, most of the Greeks left Florence and went to Venice; the Emperor followed on August 26, 1439, and in the middle of October all set sail for Constantinople.

After the departure of the Greeks, Eugene IV announced to all Christendom the happy event of the union, and ordered public prayers and processions to thank God for the great success, and to implore Him to perfect His work.

The dogmatic decision regarding the extent of the papal power, which was embodied in the Union Decree of the Council of Florence, was of extreme importance to Western Christendom, which had not yet recovered from the effects of the Western Schism. An ecumenical council had now pronounced the Pope to be the Head, not merely of individual churches, but of the Universal Church; that he derived his power, not from the will of the faithful, but immediately from Christ, whose Vicar he is, and that he is not only the Father but also the Teacher, to whom all Christians owe submission. The publication of this decision, which has become since the essential foundation of the theological development of the doctrine of the primacy of the Pope, struck a mortal blow at the very root of the schism.

Eugene IV prolonged the Council of Florence and entered into negotiations with other schismatic Orientals. In 1437 he had sent several Franciscans to the Armenians to bring about their return to the true Church. Before the Greeks departed, the Armenians arrived at Florence. After many conferences they too united with the Latin Church. The decree on the union of the Armenians Exultate

Deo was published on November 22, 1439. This decree contained the Nicene Creed, the definitions of the Councils of Chalcedon and Constantinople, also an instruction on the sacraments. This instruction on the sacraments was taken almost verbatim from the work of St. Thomas of Aquinas "on the articles of Faith and the Sacraments of the Church."

In like manner, the Jacobites of Egypt, Ethiopia and Lybia sent envoys to the Pope in Florence to bring about a union. On February 4, 1442, the decree of their union *Cantate Domino* was promulgated by the council to the whole Church.

In the fall of 1443, Eugene transferred the council from Florence to Rome, and continued to receive the Orientals into the Church. King Stephen of Bosnia made his submission; his example was followed by his relations and by the most distinguished magnates of Bosnia. Abdallah, the Syrian Patriarch of the Jacobites between the rivers Tigris and Euphrates, submitted to Rome on September 30, 1444. The Archbishop Timothy of Tarsus and the Maronite Bishop Elias of Cyprus returned to the obedience of the Roman Church on August 7, 1445.

On this date, Eugene IV published a bull, giving thanks to God that, after the return of the Greeks, Armenians and Jacobites, the Nestorians and Maronites had also paid heed to his admonitions and had solemnly professed the immutable faith of Rome.

The success obtained by Eugene IV was indeed signal, and few Popes have done so much for the Eastern Church.

XVIII
THE EIGHTEENTH ECUMENICAL COUNCIL
HELD AT THE LATERAN, ROME, 1512–1517

WORK OF THE COUNCIL: (1) The rooting out of schism; (2) the reform of the Church; (3) the Crusade against the Turks.

On October 31, 1503 Cardinal Giuliano della Rovere, practically Pope-elect, entered the Conclave together with thirty-seven other cardinals. Not many hours later his election was an accomplished fact. On the following morning, November 1, the decision of the Conclave, which had been the shortest known in the long history of the Papacy, was formally announced to the people. The newly elected Pope took the name of Julius II (1503–1513). After his election, the Pope confirmed once more the election-capitulation. Among its conditions were the waging of the war against the Turks and the restoration of discipline in the Church. To accomplish this end, it stipulated that a general council should be summoned within two years; that the Pope should not make war against any of the powers without the consent of two-thirds of the cardinals, and that the Sacred College should be consulted on all important occasions, especially in the choice of new cardinals. In order to secure the necessary freedom and safety for the next ecumenical council, the place for the meeting was to be determined by the Pope and two-thirds of the College of Cardinals. In case any impediment should be alleged to this meeting, this must be proven to the satisfaction of the same majority.

Both as a Pope and as an Italian, Julius II found himself in a most difficult position. To remain a passive spectator of confusion would have been outright abandonment of duty in a ruler and still more in a Pope. To avoid being overwhelmed by circumstances and falling helplessly into the clutches of one or the other of the great powers, it was indispensable that Julius should act at once and with decision, and if necessary take the sword into his own hands. For such a task he was admirably fitted. Disorder prevailed on all sides; the States of the Church were hardly anything more than a name. In the south, war was raging between the Spaniards and the French; in the north, Venice was taking advantage of the confusion to extend her borders at the expense of the temporal possessions of the Church.

When the Pope had finally concluded peace with Venice, thus securing the independence of the Holy See, storms arose in France and brought the Pope into conflict with Louis XII. On July 30, 1510, Louis issued a summons to all the bishops of his kingdom to send representatives from their dioceses to Orleans in September. There they were to meet and to hold a consultation on the liberties and privileges of the Gallican Church. By a royal ordinance of August 16, 1510, all French subjects were forbidden to visit the Court of Rome. The assembly met, not, however, at Orleans, but at Tours, whither Louis also betook himself.

Another and more painful surprise awaited the Pope. On May 16, 1511, a document was issued stating that the delegates of the Roman Emperor Maximilian and of the King of France proposed to summon a universal council to Pisa, to be opened on September 1, 1511. This action, in their opinion, had become necessary in order to comply with the Decree of Frequens of the Council of Constance, owing to the negligence of the Pope who had not kept the oath which he had sworn in the Conclave. They declared that the Pope's opposition to the council fully justified the action of the cardinals in thus taking the matter into their own hands. They entered beforehand a protest against all censures which the Pope might pronounce upon them. The Pope was, however, requested to attend the council either personally or through his representative. All cardinals, bishops, chapters and universities, as well as secular princes were summoned and invited to attend the council. The council was to be convoked in the name of the Cardinals Carvajal, Briconnet, Francesco Borgia, Adriano da Corneto, de Prie, Carlo del Carretto, San Severino and Ippolito D'Este. The object of the council, or, more correctly, the banners under which the forces of hypocrisy and ambition were to be marshalled, were the pacification of Christendom, a crusade against the infidels and the reform of the Church in its "Head and members." The convocation of a council under these futile pretexts by a body of schismatic cardinals was an act of open rebellion and a daring attack upon the most indisputable prerogatives of the Supreme Head of the Church. King Louis of France and Emperor Maximilian supported the refractory cardinals.

Cardinals Philip of Luxemburg, Adriano da Corneto, and Carlo del Carretto, whose names had been affixed by the other cardinals to the citation without consulting them or obtaining their permission, protested loudly against this treacherous plot and declared openly they would have nothing to do with the anti-papal council. Cardinal D'Este adopted an equivocal and compromising attitude, which finally led him to his reconciliation with Julius.

To deprive the revolting cardinals of all pretext for keeping up the schism, Julius II turned their own weapons against them for on July 25, 1511, he published a bull dated July 18, 1511, summoning a universal council to assemble in Rome on April 19, 1512. In the preamble the Pope set forth the supreme dignity of the Roman Church, sanctified by the blood of martyrs, preserved from all error, and endowed with the primacy over all churches, which entailed upon her and her Head the duty of withstanding all schismatic attempts to destroy her unity. He then declared that, both as Cardinal and Pope, he had done his best to further the convocation of a council, and that it had not been his fault that its convocation had been so long delayed. The bull continues to emphasize the point that a council can be lawfully summoned only by the Pope. Julius, then, declared that he, with the approval of the loyal cardinals and by the plenitude of his apostolic power, pronounced the edict of convocation of a synod by the revolting cardinals to be, in both its contents and effects, illegal, null and void; that its authors and their aides are deprived of all dignities, and that all cities and districts which harbor and support them are laid under interdict.

Proceedings of the Council

Opening of the Council. For three days processions of supplication were held in the Holy City, and on May 3, 1512, the council was formally opened in that venerable basilica which bears the honorable title of "Mother and Queen of all Churches." Besides Pope Julius II, sixteen cardinals were present, one hundred prelates (mostly Italians), of whom seventy were bishops, twelve patriarchs, and three generals of religious orders; in addition to these were the envoys of Spain, Venice and Florence, and a number of Roman nobles. The Mass in honor of the Holy Ghost was sung by Cardinal Riario, after which the General of the Augustinians, Giles of Viterbo, delivered an address in classical Latin, which the members of the council universally applauded. Then the Pope bestowed the solemn benediction and announced a plenary indulgence. After the customary prayers, Cardinal Farnese read the Pope's address, in which Julius set forth the reasons which inspired him to summon the council. When the introductory ceremonies were concluded, the Pope fixed the tenth of May as the day of the first session.

First Session (May 10, 1512). The session took place under the presidency of the Pope; Cardinal Grimani sang the Mass and Bernardino Zane preached the sermon. In his sermon the latter touched first and briefly on the Turkish danger and then proceeded to treat of the unity of the Church. Unity he defined as consisting: (1) in the union of the members with each other; (2) in their subordination to the Head, the Vicar of Christ; hence all members who do not obey the Head and who separate themselves from the other members of the body, are thereby schismatics. The Pope then delivered a short address, in which he stated the objects of the council. He described these as (1) *The rooting out of schism;* (2) *the reform of the Church;* (3) *the Crusade against the Turks.*

Second Session (May 17, 1512). The High Mass was sung by the Hungarian Cardinal, Thomas Backocs, and a very remarkable sermon was preached by the General of the Dominicans, Thomas de Vio (Cajetan). His subject was the Catholic doctrine regarding the Church and synods. He described the Church as the Holy City of Jerusalem seen by St. John (Apoc. 21:1), with her healing powers (the sacraments), her apostles, pastors, teachers and gifts, and expounded the close, mutual union existing among her inhabitants like that union which exists between all the members of the same body. This Church, he went on to say, is governed by the Vicar of Christ, and to him all her citizens owe allegiance. The Pisan Synod possessed not one of the notes of the true Church. It was neither holy nor lawfully convoked; in fact, it was stained with error for it subordinated the Pope to the Church and set the members above the Head.

At the conclusion of Cajetan's address a letter from the King of England professing his alliance with the Pope was read; and another from the King of Spain.

The reading of the papal bull followed next, confirming and renewing the censures which the Pope had pronounced against the pseudo-Council of Pisa.

Third Session (December 3, 1512). One hundred and eleven members, under the presidency of Julius II, attended the session. The High Mass was sung by Cardinal Vigerio and the sermon was preached by the Bishop of Melfi, his subject being the unity of the Church. After this the Secretary of the Council read a letter from Emperor Maximilian, in which he repudiated the pseudo-Council set up by the King of France, first at Tours, and afterwards at Pisa. Maximilian declared his adherence to the Lateran Council. At the close of the session the Bishop of Forli read a papal bull which declared again that all the acts of the Pisan Synod were null and void and pronounced the interdict on France.

Fourth Session (December 10, 1512). Nineteen cardinals, ninety-six patriarchs, archbishops and bishops, four abbots and four generals of religious orders were present under the presidency of the Pope. The Pope ordered the Secretary to read the letters patent, whereby Louis XI, King of France, had abrogated the *Pragmatic Sanction of Bourges.*

(Charles VII, in an assembly of bishops and nobles at Bourges, in 1448, issued an edict known as the *Pragmatic Sanction of Bourges.* In it the King declared that a general council was superior to the Pope, suppressed the revenues gathered for the Court of Rome, and denied that the Pope had the right to nominate bishops and abbots in France. This sanction had been abolished by Louis XI on November 27, 1461. Louis XII, to spite the Pope, re-introduced it in France.)

After the reading of the abolition of the *Pragmatic Sanction,* a warning was issued to France, which summoned all protagonists of the Sanction in France, whether they be laymen or ecclesiastics, to appear before the council within sixty days to give an account of their conduct.

Fifth Session (February 16, 1513). A bull was read, confirming former papal decrees on the *Pragmatic Sanction.* The address at this session, the last at which Julius II was present, was delivered by the Apostolic Notary, Marcellus of Venice, and was an enthusiastic panegyric on the Pope.

On February 21, 1513, Julius II passed away, clear and conscious to the last. Rome felt that the soul which had passed from her had been of royal cast. Julius was succeeded on March 11, 1513, by the Cardinal Deacon John de Medici, who assumed the name of Leo X (1513–1521).

Sixth Session (April 27, 1513). Pope Leo X presided. The new Pope addressed the members of the synod and declared his resolve to continue the council until it had secured complete peace for Christendom.

Seventh Session (June 17, 1513). The Cardinals Carvajal and San Severino repudiated the Synod of Pisa, recognized the Lateran Council, and asked for absolution from the censure they had incurred. There was a long discussion before this favor was granted to them. Leo hoped, and rightly so, to destroy schism by gentleness rather than by severity. He proposed to them a form of abjuration, after the reading and signing of which the Pope pronounced their absolution, and received them back into the Sacred College. For penance they received the obligation of fasting once a week for the rest of their lives.

Eighth Session (December 19, 1513). Besides the Pope, twenty-three cardinals, eleven archbishops, forty-five bishops, five generals of religious orders and many envoys were present. The ambassadors of Louis XII presented his renunciation of the Synod of Pisa, then in session at Lyons, and his recognition of the Lateran Council. In this session, Leo X published the bull *Apostolici Regiminis*, which condemned the doctrine that the soul of man is mortal, and also the teaching that one and the same soul is in all men. "De anima humana (contra Neo-Aristotelicos): Cum diebus nostris (quod dolenter referimus) zizaniae seminator, antiquus humani generis hostis, nonnullos perniciosissimos errores, a fidelibus semper explosos, in agro Domini superseminare et augere sit ausus, de natura praesertim animae rationalis, quod videlicet mortalis sit, aut unica in cunctis hominibus, et nonnulli temere philosophantes, secundum saltem philosophiam verum id esse asseverent contra hujusmodi pestem opportuna remedia adhibere cupientes, hoc sacro approbante Concilio damnamus et reprobamus omnes asserentes, animam intellectivam mortalem esse, aut unicam in cunctis hominibus."

It was resolved to send legates to all Christian sovereigns to implore them to turn their arms against the Turks.

Ninth Session (May 5, 1514). The absent French bishops were charged with contumacy; after it had been shown that these prelates had started on their journey to the council, but had been detained by the Duke of Milan, Pope Leo extended the time allowed for their appearance at the council.

Tenth Session (May 4, 1515). Two decrees of capital importance were passed at this session: the first gave sanction to the *"Monti di Pietà"*—*"Mountains* (Institutions) *of Benevolence";* the other concerned the printing of books.

As in the thirteenth century, so in the latter half of the fifteenth century, it was the Franciscans who, with the sanction of the Holy See, took the social reform in hand. Their contacts with all classes of society had rendered them familiar with the pitiless greed with which Jewish money-lenders took advantage of a temporary embarrassment of the impoverished to demand incredibly high interest. To prevent this oppressive exploitation of the needs of the smaller townsfolk and of the poor, the Franciscans resolved to found institutions where any one in want of ready money could obtain it in exchange for some pledge and without interest. The working capital of the scheme would be supplied by voluntary contributions, gifts and legacies; hence the name *"Monti di Pietà"*—*"Mountains* (Institutions) *of Benevolence."* The first of these charitable institutions was opened in the Papal States; in Orvieto in 1463, and in Perugia in 1461. In both places the Franciscans were the originators of the plan. In fact, such great saints of the order, as St. Bernardine of Siena, St. John Capistrano and St. James della Marchia were indefatigable supporters and workers for these institutions. In the course of time similar benevolent banks were opened in Assisi, Mantua, Pavia, Ravenna, Verona, Ferrara, Parma, Rimini, and in many other places. Blessed Bernardine of

Monte Feltro, a famous Franciscan missionary, was especially untiring in this work. The extraordinary and rapid growth and spread of these institutions—to France, England, Bavaria—are the best proofs that they responded to a real want. The grinding usury practiced by the Jews was almost incredible. In Florence they exacted 32½% interest for loans; in some other places they demanded as high as 40% interest. The ever-increasing demands upon the Monti di Pietà necessarily entailed a corresponding increase in the expenses of administration. Thus it was found necessary to make a small charge on each loan in order to cover these expenses. To this plan the Dominicans objected. A literary controversy arose on this question, but at last the Franciscans won out. The foundation of these institutions had been approved by Popes Pius II, Paul II, Sixtus IV, Innocent VIII and Julius II.

Leo X in this tenth session of the council approved of the Monti di Pieta and permitted the demand of a small percentage of interest on loans, sufficient to defray the expenses of the management, but there was to be no profit in the transaction. And any one who asserted this to be unlawful thereby incurred excommunication. The decree of the council reads: "Sacro approbante Concilio, declaramus et definimus, *'Montes pietatis'* per respublicas institutos et auctoritate Sedis Apostolicae hactenus probatos et confirmatos, in quibus pro eorum impensis et indemnitate aliquid moderatum ad solas ministrorum impensas et aliarum rerum ad illorum conservationem, ut praefertur, pertinentium, pro eorum indemnitate dumtaxat, ultra sortem absque lucro eorundem Montium recipitur, neque speciem mali praeferre, nec peccandi incentivum praestare, neque ullo pacto improbari, quin immo meritorium esse ac laudari et probari debere tale mutuum et minime usurarium putari... Omnes autem religiosos et ecclesiasticas ac saeculares personas, qui contra praesentis declarationis et sanctionis formam de cetero praedicare seu disputare verbo vel scriptis ausi fuerint, excommunicationis latae sententiae poenam, privilegio quocunque non obstante, incurrere volumus."

In the other decree the Pope forbids, with the approval of the council, under pain of excommunication and imposition of heavy fines, the printing of books without the approbation of the bishop of the diocese and the inquisitor, and in Rome, of the Cardinal Vicar and the Master of the Palace. Every book printed contrary to these regulations shall be burned.

Yet another weighty question came up: the reform of the calendar. The opinions, however, were so divergent that Leo X had to withdraw the question from the business of the tenth session as not yet ripe for action.

Eleventh Session (December 19, 1516). The envoys of Simon Peter, Patriarch of the Maronites of the Lebanon, were admitted to tender their obedience to the Pope. The Patriarch's letter contained a profession of faith, wherein the Maronites avowed their belief in the procession of the Holy Ghost from the Father *and the Son;* in the doctrine of purgatory and in Easter Communion. The Patriarch thanked the Pope for having sent the Guardian of the Franciscan Monastery at Beyrut to instruct the Maronites. A *concordat* made between the Pope and the King of France was next read to the council. Then followed the reading of the bull *Pastor aeternus,* which abrogated the *Pragmatic Sanction.*

Twelfth Session (March 16, 1517). A bull was read to the effect that there was no need of prolonging the Lateran Council since peace had been now established among Christian Princes; the reform of morals had been attended to by salutary canons, and the Schism of Pisa had been abolished. An imposition of tithes on all benefices was ordered; these tithes were to be used for a war against the Turks.

Many assert that the closing of the Lateran Council was premature in view of the tempest which broke loose on the following October 31, 1517. Certainly Leo X had good reasons for closing the council. If the Lateran Council fell short of a "root-and-branch reform," it produced many opportune and salutary laws, on which the Council of Trent was able afterwards to enlarge and improve.

XIX
THE NINETEENTH ECUMENICAL COUNCIL
HELD AT TRENT 1545–1563

WORK OF THE COUNCIL: Extirpation of heresy (against the innovators of the 16th century), and reform of morals.

For more than a century and a half reform of the Church "in its Head and members" was the watchword both of the friends and the enemies of religion. Earnest men looked forward to it as the only means of stemming the tide of neo-paganism which threatened to engulf the Christian world, while wicked men hoped to find in the movement for reform an opportunity for wrecking the divine constitution which Christ had given to His Church. Popes and councils had failed hitherto to accomplish the much-needed reform. The bishops had met at Constance and Basel, at Florence and at Rome, and had parted, leaving the root of evil untouched. Notwithstanding all these failures, the feeling was practically universal that in a general council lay the only hope of reform. For one reason or another the Roman Curia looked with an unfavorable eye on the convocation of such an assembly.

The hesitation of Hadrian VI (1522–1523) and of Clement VII (1523–1534) to yield to the demands for an ecumenical council was due neither to their inability to appreciate the magnitude of the abuses nor to their desire to oppose any and every proposal for reform. The disturbed condition of the times, when so many individuals had fallen away from the faith, and when whole nations formerly noted for their loyalty to the Pope threatened to follow in the footsteps of individuals, made it difficult to decide whether the suggested remedy might not prove worse than the disease. The memory, too, of the scenes which took place at Constance and Basel, and of the revolutionary proposals which were put forward in these assemblies, made the Pope less anxious to try a similar experiment with the possibility of even worse results, particularly at the time when the unfriendly relations existing between the Empire, France and England held out little hope for the success of a general council. As events showed, the delay was providential. It afforded an opportunity for the excitement and passion to die away; it helped to secure moderation in the views and it allowed the issues in dispute to shape themselves more clearly, and to be narrowed down to their true proportions, thereby enabling the Catholic theologians to formulate precisely the doctrines of the Church in opposition to the opinions of the Lutherans.

It was only on the accession of Paul III (1534–1549) to the Chair of St. Peter, that a really vigorous effort was made to undertake the work of reform. He signalized his pontificate by the stern measures he took to reform the Roman Curia; then, by the appointment of learned and progressive ecclesiastics, like Reginald Pole, Sadoleto, Cantarini, to the College of Cardinals, and by the establishment of special tribunals to combat heresy.

After a preliminary agreement with Emperor Charles V (1519–1556), Paul III convoked a general council and ordered it to meet at Mantua in 1537; but the refusal of the Lutherans to send representatives to the council, the prohibition issued by Francis I (1515–1547), King of France, forbidding the French bishops to attend, and the unwillingness of the Duke of Mantua to make the necessary arrangements for such an assembly in his territory, made it necessary to prorogue the council to Vincenza in 1538. But because only a few bishops had arrived at the place and time appointed, the council was adjourned, at first, but later on prorogued indefinitely. Negotiations were, however, continued regarding the place of the future assembly. The Pope was anxious that the council should be held in an Italian city, while Charles V, believing that the Lutherans would never consent to go to Italy, or to accept the decrees of an Italian assembly, insisted that a German city should be selected. In the end, as a compromise, Trent was agreed upon by both parties. Then the council was convoked once more to meet in Trent in 1542. The refusal of the Lutherans to take part in the proposed council, the unwillingness of Francis I to permit any of the bishops to be present, and the threatened war between France and the Empire, made it impossible for the council to meet at the specified time. Finally, at the conclusion of the Peace of Crespy (1544), which put an end to the war with France the council was again convoked to meet at Trent in March 1545. The Cardinal Bishop John Maria del Monte, the Cardinal Priest Marcellus Cervini, and the Cardinal Deacon Reginald Pole were appointed to represent the Pope. When the day (March 15, 1545) fixed for the opening ceremony had arrived, a further adjournment of the council was rendered imperative, owing to the sparse attendance of bishops.

On May 3, 1545, the legates called together the ten bishops who had appeared in Trent, and communicated to them the papal orders and the reasons for the temporary delay. In a consistory, held on November 6, 1545, it was finally settled that the opening of the council should take place on the third Sunday in Advent, December 13, 1545. The universal longing of many years, the event around which so many baffled hopes had centered, was on the point of realization.

Proceedings of the Council
first period, 1545–1549*

On receiving the papal brief giving orders for the opening of the council, the legates immediately appointed a day of fast and prescribed that processions be held on December 12, 1545. They proclaimed an indulgence for those who received the sacraments under the usual conditions. Paul III, in a special bull, ordered universal supplications and processions to invoke God's blessing upon the council. In Rome, these processions were held on December 14, 15, 16, 1545.

First Session (December 13, 1545). The bishops assembled with the legates in the church of the Most Blessed Trinity, and thence proceeded in copes and mitres to the cathedral, accompanied by the clergy of the city, singing the "Veni,

Creator." The choir of the cathedral had been fitted up as the council hail. The senior President of the Council, Cardinal del Monte, celebrated the solemn Mass in honor of the Holy Ghost, and granted a plenary indulgence to those present. Bishop Cornelius Mussi of Bitonto, a renowned Franciscan orator, then mounted the pulpit and preached a Latin sermon, in which he gave his enthusiasm free course. After Cardinal del Monte had said the prayers prescribed by the Ceremonial, Bishop Thomas Campeggio of Feltre read the bull: *Laetare Jerusalem* (Rejoice Jerusalem) of November 19, 1544, and the bull of February 22, 1545, in which the cardinal legates were nominated. Finally, Cardinal del Monte, with the assent of the bishops, declared the council officially open. He appointed January 7, 1546 for the second session. The ceremonies ended with the singing of the *Te Deum*. Present at the opening session, besides the three papal legates, were Cardinal Madruzzo of Trent, four archbishops, twenty-one bishops, five generals of religious orders. The theologians present at this session included four secular priests from Spain; the remaining were regulars, namely, six Dominicans, eighteen Franciscans, five Augustinian Hermits, five Carmelites, and four Servites.

Three general congregations, occupied with the organization and procedure of the council, prepared the way for the second session. The important question whether dogma or reform was to be discussed first in the council was brought up before the bishops, and made the subject of debate. As differences of opinions manifested themselves, a decision was postponed for the time being. The question of the right to vote also came up for discussion; some wished this right to be vested exclusively in the bishops, others wished the decision be deferred until the council had a larger attendance. Cardinal del Monte carried his point that the generals of religious orders should also enjoy the right to vote. After long discussion it was decided that the three Benedictine abbots, sent by the Pope, should have one vote collectively, and that each general of a religious order should have a vote for his respective order.

Another debate arose on the title of the council. Several bishops proposed that to the title *"Holy Synod of Trent"* should be added: *"representing the Universal Church."* This proposal met with special and vigorous opposition from Cardinals del Monte and Madruzzo. The former showed that it was uncalled for, to imitate the precedents of Constance and Basel; the latter pointed out that this magniloquent title would only irritate the Protestants. The majority were in favor of rejecting this title.

Second Session (January 7, 1546). After the usual prayers and ceremonies the Secretary of the Council, Massarelli, read an impressive exhortation, composed by Cardinal Pole, from the legates to the fathers. In eloquent terms this document described the corruption of the Church, and exhorted the fathers to amendment and contrition of heart, whereby alone they could expect the descent of the Holy Spirit upon themselves and their work. Besides the three legates and the Cardinal of Trent there were present four archbishops, twenty-eight bishops, five generals of religious orders and three abbots.

In the interval between the second and third sessions six general congregations were held, in which the title of the council gave rise to prolonged discussions. After many deliberations the fathers agreed to treat dogma and reform simultaneously.

Third Session (February 4, 1546). The profession of faith was made by all present "Haec sacrosancta oecumenica et generalis Tridentina Synodus, in Spiritu Sancto legitime congregata… Symbolum fidei, quo sancta Romana Ecclesia utitur, tanquam principium illud, in quo omnes, qui fidem Christi profitentur, necessario conveniunt, ad fundamentum firmum et unicum, contra quod 'portae inferi nunquam praevalebunt' (Matth, xvi, 18) totidem verbis, quibus in omnibus ecclesiis legitur, exprimendum esse censuit. Quod quidem ejusmodi est: (sequitur Symbolum Nicaeno Constantinopolitanum)." "This holy ecumenical and general Synod of Trent, legitimately assembled in the Holy Spirit, is of the belief that there should be given expression to a symbol of Faith which the holy Roman Church uses, as that principle, on which all who profess the faith of Christ, must necessarily agree, conformable to the firm and only foundation, against which 'the gates of hell shall never prevail' (Mt. 16:18) with so many words as it is read in all churches. And this is of this tenor (Here follows the Nicene-Constantinopolitan Creed)."

The council also settled the official title: Sacrosancta oecumenica et universalis Tridentina Synodus, in Spiritu Sancto legitime congregata. "The Holy Ecumenical and General Synod of Trent, legitimately assembled in the Holy Spirit." Present at this session were five cardinals, six archbishops, twenty-six bishops, four generals of religious orders and three abbots.

The attitude of the Protestants towards the council was anything but encouraging, and Luther's death, which occurred on February 18, 1546, did not improve the situation. Melanchthon issued a pamphlet opposing the council; and soon afterwards two long pamphlets were printed by the Protestants, rejecting the council.

Fourth Session (April 8, 1546). The first decree on the Canonical Scriptures declared that not only the books of the Old and New Testament, but also the Apostolic Tradition are the source of faith in the Church. Then the council enumerates all the Books of each Testament. The abuses which had become current in regard to editions and translations of the Holy Books, as well as in regard to their interpretation and use, led to the second decree of "the editions and use of the Sacred Books." The council declared that the ancient Latin version, known as *Vulgate*, used by the Church for so many centuries, is the authentic edition, and, therefore, must be used in public lectures, disputations, sermons and expositions, and no one should dare, under any pretext whatever, to reject it. It was further ordained that in the future no books on religious subjects could be printed, if the name of the author is omitted, nor could they be sold or kept, if they have not been examined and approved by the bishop beforehand. Present at this session were five cardinals, eight archbishops, forty-one bishops, four generals of religious orders and three abbots.

Fifth Session (June 17, 1546). The decree on *"Original Sin,"* its nature, its propagation, its consequences, and its remission in baptism was published. The council declared that it was not its intention to include in this decree on Original Sin the Blessed and Immaculate Virgin and Mother of God. It upheld the decision of the Franciscan Pope Sixtus IV, who in 1475 issued an Office of the Immaculate Conception of the Blessed Virgin Mary. "Declarat haec ipsa sancta Synodus, non esse suae intentionis, comprehendere in hoc decreto, ubi de peccato originali agitur, beatam et immaculatam Virginem Mariam Dei genetricem, sed observandas esse constitutiones felicis recordationis Sixti Papae IV, sub poenis in eis constitutionibus contentis, quas innovat." The Franciscan and the Jesuit, Laynez and Salmeron were the champions of Mary's "exemption" from the decree on Original Sin, while the Dominicans argued against it to the end. The reform decree dealt with Holy Scripture, demanding expert instruction in the same, and regulated the preaching of the Word of God. Present at this session were four cardinals, nine archbishops, forty-eight bishops, three generals of religious orders and two abbots.

Sixth Session (January 13, 1547). This was one of the most important sessions of the council; the decree on *"Justification"* was published. After repeated drafts, redrafts and alterations, after thorough and impartial discussions, the decree on Justification, composed with scrupulous care, was finally published. It consists of sixteen chapters and thirty-three canons. It is a masterpiece of theology, formulating with clearness and precision the Catholic doctrine as distinguished from the Pelagian errors, on the one hand, and from the Protestant errors, on the other. The General of the Augustinian Hermits, Seripando, the Franciscan and Jesuit theologians, together with Cardinal del Monte, were the chief framers of the decree on Justification. The reform decree of this session dealt with episcopal residence. Present at it were four cardinals, ten archbishops, forty-five bishops, five generals of religious orders and two abbots.

Seventh Session (March 3, 1547). The council passed thirteen dogmatic canons on the *"Sacraments"* in general; fourteen canons on *"Baptism"*; three canons on *"Confirmation"*. The reform decree dealt with the life of the bishops, the exemption of regulars, and the holding of ecclesiastical benefices. Present at this session were four cardinals, nine archbishops, fifty-two bishops, five generals of religious orders and two abbots.

Eighth Session (March 11, 1547). In this session Cardinal del Monte made known the ascertained facts of the plague which had broken out in Trent. He then read a decree on the transfer of the council; a vote was taken and a majority of two-thirds were found to be in favor of transferring the council to Bologna. Del Monte now informed the fathers of the council that the legates had from the very beginning been empowered by a papal bull to transfer the council, should necessity arise.

Ninth Session (April 21, 1547). The council, now meeting in Bologna, passed decrees on the *"Holy Eucharist"* and *"Penance"*. Three cardinals, six bishops, four generals of religious orders and one abbot were in attendance.

Tenth Session (June 2, 1547). The subject matter of the previous session was continued. Three cardinals, eight archbishops, sixty-nine bishops, six generals of religious orders and two abbots were present.

The council was officially suspended on November 17, 1549. Pope Paul III, who has won undying fame by his unceasing and untiring work in behalf of the council, died on November 10, 1549.

SECOND PERIOD, 1551–1552

In casting a glance over the fifteen years of the pontificate of Paul III, the conviction is forced upon us that the dawn of a new era, full of hope, had arisen for the Church, in which she would again, as so often before, gloriously establish her spiritual ascendancy and her marvelous power of rejuvenation. The externally brilliant, but essentially worldly, period of the Renaissance, which took Church and religion as lightly as it did life itself, was hurrying towards its end. However much Paul III paid tribute to the fearful epoch in which he had come to power, he was nevertheless just to that generation in which the strictly ecclesiastical element, never losing sight of its goal, was working towards a reform of conditions that were utterly corrupt, and was striving to cope with a dangerous crisis by means of an entirely new state of things. The inauguration of the Council of Trent, the removal of abuses, and the renewal of the College of Cardinals were all of epoch-making importance.

After the death of Paul III the Church remained for nearly three months without a Head. The cause of this unusual delay is to be found rather in the behaviour of the secular princes, who interfered in the most unjustifiable manner in the electoral discussions, than in the party deliberations of the College of Cardinals, and the great number of candidates. The Conclave began on November 29, 1549, and finished only on February 8, 1550, when Cardinal del Monte was elected; he assumed the name of Julius III (1550–1555). Among the points of the election capitulation to which Julius III had pledged himself in the Conclave, the re-opening of the Council of Trent for the extirpation of heresy and the reform of the Church stood in the first place. For the promotion of this promise the Pope entered upon diplomatic negotiations with Charles V and Henry II immediately after his accession to the papal chair.

Regardless of the political situation, which grew darker from day to day, Julius continued his preparations for the council, which he was determined to open in spite of every difficulty. In a bull, carefully prepared and adopted in a secret consistory, Julius III announced his intention of laboring for the peace of the Church, the spread of the Christian Faith, and of providing, as far as lay in his power, for the tranquillity of Germany. As it was his right, in virtue of his office, the Pope addressed to the patriarchs, bishops, abbots, and all upon whom it may be incumbent to assist at a general council of the Church, the earnest admonition and invitation to repair to the city of Trent on the coming first of May, for the re-opening of the council; should he be prevented from presiding in person, the papal legates would be there on the appointed date.

The legates of the council, Crescenzi, Pighino, and Hippomano, made their solemn entry into Trent on April 29, 1551. Cardinal Madruzzo of Trent, four archbishops and nine bishops welcomed them. Cardinal Crescenzi declared that in accordance with the will of the Pope, the council must open on May 1.

RE-OPENING OF THE COUNCIL

Eleventh Session (May 1, 1551). This session, the first held under Pope Julius III, was very poorly attended. After a solemn High Mass celebrated by Cardinal Crescenzi, the Franciscan Sigismond Fedrio of Diruta preached the sermon. After the sermon the Secretary of the Council, Massarelli, read the papal bull, summoning the council, and the brief, nominating the presidents. Announcement was made that the next session would not take place till September 1, so that the Germans might have time to appear in Trent. On the same day, May 1, the Pope had gone in solemn procession from St. Mark to the Church of the Holy Apostles in Rome, where a Mass was celebrated in honor of the Holy Ghost for the happy issue of the council.

Although the Emperor showed great zeal for the furtherance of the council, the prospects for the assembly still looked very gloomy; for Henry II of France worked deliberately against the assembly. He broke off diplomatic relations with the Pope at the beginning of July, and his ambassador made a formal protest against the council.

Twelfth Session (September 1, 1551). The three Presidents, Cardinal Madruzzo, two prince-electors, five other archbishops, twenty-six bishops and twenty-five theologians assembled for this session. High Mass was celebrated by the Archbishop of Cagliari, and instead of a sermon, the Secretary of the Council read a long admonition, written by the Presidents, and addressed to those assembled. It was decided that the Sacrament of Holy Eucharist and the duty of residence of the bishops should be dealt with at the next session on October 11th.

The bishops assembled in Trent resumed their activities at once after the twelfth session. On September 2, ten articles concerning the Eucharist, taken from the writings of Luther and the Swiss reformers, were laid before the theologians of the council for examination. The theologians were enjoined to base their reasons on the Holy Scriptures, on apostolic tradition, on lawful councils, on the Fathers of the Church, on the constitutions of the Popes and on the consensus of the Universal Church. In so doing they were to avoid all haste, as well as all unnecessary discussions and contentious disputations. Cardinal Crescenzi urged especially that they should limit themselves to a clear setting forth of the errors and not venture on theological sarcasm. During the deliberations the question of the chalice for the laity and of children's Communion were minutely discussed.

Thirteenth Session (October 11, 1551). This session took place with unusual solemnity. The three Presidents, Cardinal Madruzzo, three prince-electors, five archbishops, thirty-four bishops, five generals of religious orders, three abbots, forty-eight theologians, as well as several ambassadors, took part in this session.

In the decree dealing with the *"Holy Eucharist,"* the Catholic doctrine concerning this Sacrament, the greatest of the treasures of the Church, to the glorification of which Raphael had created the immortal fresco of the *"Disputa,"* is set forth with admirable lucidity.

"Although our Saviour," teaches the council, "in his natural existence is always at the right hand of the Father in heaven, he is still, in his substance, present in many places in a sacramental manner." "Ut Salvator foster semper ad dextram Patris in coelis assideat juxta modum existendi naturalem et multis nihilominus aliis in locis sacramentaliter praesens sua substantia nobis adsit" (Chap. 1). "By the consecration, the substance of the bread and the substance of the wine are changed into the substance of the Body and Blood of Christ our Lord. And this change is rightly and fittingly called *'Transubstantiation'* by the Holy Catholic Church. Sancta haec Synodus declarat: "Per consecrationem panis et vini conversionem fieri totius substantiae panis in substantiam corporis Christi Domini nostri, et totius substantiae vini in substantiam sanguinis ejus. Quae conversio convenienter et proprie a sancta catholic Ecclesia *'Transubstantiatio'* est appellata" (Chap. 4). "The Church has always believed that immediately after the consecration Christ our Lord is present, with body and soul, with Divinity and Humanity under the appearances of bread and wine, and also in every particle of the same." "Semper haec fides in Ecclesia Dei fuit, statim post consecrationem verum Domini nostri corpus verumque ejus sanguinem sub panis et vini specie una cum ipsius anima et divinitate exsistere... Totus integer Christus sub panis specie et sub quavis ipsius speciei parte, totus item sub vini specie et sub ejus partibus exsistit" (Chap. 3). It is further emphasized that Christ is not only present at the moment of participation, but also before and after. "Si quis dixerit, peracta consecratione in admirabili Eucharistiae Sacramento non esse corpus et sanguinem Domini nostri Jesu Christi, sed tantum in usu, dum sumitur, non autem ante vel post, et in hostiis consecratis, quae post communionem reservantur vel supersunt, non remanere verum corpus Domini: anathema sit" (Canon 4). Concerning the preparation for Holy Communion, the Council expressly declares that no one, conscious of mortal sin, should dare to approach the Holy Sacrament without having previously confessed (Canon 11). With regard to the effects the Council teaches that the Holy Eucharist blots out our daily sins and preserves us from mortal sin, that it is a food for our souls, and a pledge of a future life, so that we should often partake of this Bread of the Angels (Chapter 2).

The reform decree, consisting of eight chapters, dealt mainly with the authority of the bishops in their dioceses, with jurisdiction, with the procedure of an appeal to the Pope, and similar matters relating to the ecclesiastical government of the Church.

Fourteenth Session (November 25, 1551). In this session the council published twelve dogmatic chapters on the Sacraments of *"Penance"* and *"Extreme Unction"* and nineteen canons condemning the heretical teachings of the reformers in regard to these sacraments.

Regarding the sacrament of penance the council teaches—in fifteen canons—that it was instituted by Christ, that it differs from baptism, that it is a necessary means of reconciliation with God for every one who has committed mortal sin after baptism; that the penitent must have contrition which is defined as a sorrow of the soul and hatred of sins committed, with the purpose of sinning no more; that he must make the confession of all his mortal sins, and make due satisfaction for them. By confession of sins, which is ordained by God, he Church demands nothing further from the penitent than that he should confess all those mortal sins which he remembers after a diligent examination of conscience. Absolution is *not a mere declaration* that the sins are forgiven, *it is an official act,* by which, the priest pronounces sentence as a judge. The power of giving absolution is possessed by every priest validly ordained, even if he should be in the state of mortal sin, provided he possesses either ordinary or delegated jurisdiction. Regarding satisfaction, it is emphasized that the temporal punishment due to sin, is not fully remitted by absolution. "Si quis dixerit, fictionem esse, quod, virtute clavium sublata poena aeterna, poena temporalis plerumque exsolvenda remaneat, anathema sit." "If any one should say that it is fiction, that after the eternal punishment has been taken away by the power of the keys, the temporal punishment often remains to be paid, let him be anathema" (Canon 15).

In dealing with extreme unction—in four canons—the council emphasizes above all things that it is a real sacrament, instituted by Jesus Christ.

The reform decree, which contained fourteen chapters, was drawn up principally with the intention of regulating clerical life and dress.

At the fourteenth session were present, besides the three presidents, Cardinal Madruzzo, six archbishops, forty bishops, one general, five abbots, six procurators, three dukes and fifty-one theologians.

Fifteenth Session (January 25, 1552). The Catholic doctrine on the Holy Sacrifice of the Mass and the ordination of priests was to be published in this session. A commission of eighteen prelates had drawn up four chapters of instruction and thirteen canons on the Holy Mass and three chapters of instruction and eight canons on holy orders. The publication of these decrees did not take place in this session, nor during the second period of the council. In order to do everything possible on his part to win over the Protestants, the legate declared himself ready to comply with the wish of those Protestants who had come to Trent, to postpone the decrees already prepared on the Sacrifice of the Mass and holy orders until March 19th.

At this (15th) session, the decree of adjournment, as well as the new letter of safe-conduct for the Protestants, were made public. This letter afforded to all Germans, and in particular to all the adherents of the *"Confession of Augsburg,"* the fullest security in coming to Trent, in staying there, in making proposals, in negotiating with the council, in presenting any article of the Creed in writing or orally, supporting the same with passages taken from Holy Scripture and the Holy Fathers. The Protestants were finally assured that they would not be punished on account of their religion; that they would be at perfect liberty to return home when it pleased them; that they could leave the city and return to it at their own discretion. Some representatives of Protestant princes were, however, not yet satisfied with this exhaustive letter of safe-conduct.

On March 20, news reached Rome that the whole of Germany was in arms, and there was no longer any doubt as to the alliance made between the French King and the Protestant princes. It seemed certain that to continue the council in view of the existing state of affairs would be highly dangerous. The Pope, however, in spite of this alarming news, still hesitated until the middle of April to suspend the council. His decision was made imperative by the news that Augsburg had fallen into the hands of the enemies of Charles V, whereby the safety of Trent was greatly threatened. Julius III, after due deliberation with the cardinals, decided to suspend the council on April 15th, in order to obviate the danger of the council dissolving itself.

Sixteenth Session (April 28, 1552). The decree of suspension was published. Twelve prelates, mostly Spanish, protested against it. They remained in Trent, but were compelled to make a hasty exit, when the Ehrenber mountain pass was captured by Maurice of Saxony. The legate, Cardinal Crescenzi, went from Trent to Verona on May 26th, where he died on May 28th.

The council was suspended for two years. If, however, a propitious time for resuming the council should come before the lapse of two years, the council was to take up its work immediately.

THIRD PERIOD, 1562–1563

On the death of Julius III, Marcellus II succeeded to the Papacy, but his reign was cut short by death (he reigned twenty-two days). In the Conclave which followed, Cardinal Peter Caraffa, the first General and in a certain sense the founder of the Theatines, received the required majority of votes, notwithstanding the express veto of the Emperor. He was proclaimed Pope under the name of Paul IV (1555–1559). The new Pope had been remarkable for his stern views, his ascetic life, and his adherence to the scholastic as opposed to humanist views. As nuncio in Spain he had acquired a complete distrust of the Spanish rulers. The unfriendly relations existing between Paul IV and Philip II of Spain (1555–1598), the husband of Mary I, Queen of England (1553–1558), rendered difficult the work of bringing about a complete reconciliation between England and the Holy See.

Owing to the disturbed condition of Europe, and the attitude of the Emperor and the King of Spain, it would have been impossible for the Pope, even had he been anxious to do so, to re-convoke the council. He would not so much as even consider the idea of selecting Trent or any German city as a fit place for such an assembly. But of his own initiative he took strong measures to reform the Roman Curia, established a special commission in Rome to assist him in this work, and presided frequently at the meetings of the Inquisition. He had been beloved at first by the Romans on account of his economic administration, whereby the taxes were reduced considerably, but the disastrous results of the war against Philip II in Naples effaced the memory of the benefits he had conferred, and he died, detested by the people.

In the conclave which followed, the two great parties among the cardinals were the French and the Austro-Spanish, neither of which, however, was strong enough to procure the election of its nominee. After a struggle, lasting three months, Cardinal John Angelus de Medici was elected by acclamation, and assumed the name of Pius IV (1559–1565). The new Pope had nothing of the stern, morose temperament of his predecessor. He was of a mild disposition, and anxious to advance the interests of religion by kindness rather than by severity. He was determined to proceed at all cost with the work of the council, and as a first step in that direction he devoted all his energies to the establishment of friendly relations with Emperor Ferdinand I (1556–1564) and with Spain. In all his ambitions for reform he was loyally supported by his nephew, St. Charles Borromeo, whom he created cardinal, and to whom he entrusted the work of preparing the measures which should be submitted to the future council.

When all arrangements had been made, the bull of reconvocation, summoning the bishops to meet at Trent at Easter 1561, was published on November 29, 1560. Though it was not expressly stated in the document, yet it was implied clearly enough, that the assembly was not to be a new council, but only the continuation of the Council of Trent. This was not satisfactory to France, which demanded a revision of some of the decrees passed previously at Trent, and objected strongly to the selection of Trent as the meeting place. The Emperor Ferdinand I and King Philip II expressed their anxiety to further the project of the Pope. Delegates were sent from Rome to interview the Lutheran princes and theologians, but everywhere they met with sharp rebuffs. In an assembly held at Naumburg in 1561, the Lutherans refused to attend the council unless they were admitted on their own terms, while many of the Catholic princes and bishops showed no inclination to respond to the papal convocation.

The Pope appointed Cardinal Hercules Gonzaga the first President of the council, together with Cardinal Hosius, Bishop of Ermland, Jerome Seripando, Archbishop of Salerno, Louis Simonetta of Milan and Mark of Altemps. When the legates arrived in Trent on April 16, 1561, to open the council, they found so few bishops in attendance that they could do nothing but prepare the subjects to be submitted for future discussion.

RE-OPENING OF THE COUNCIL

Seventeenth Session (January 18, 1562). Besides the legates, three patriarchs, eleven archbishops, forty bishops, four generals of religious orders and four abbots attended the session. From the very beginning the legates found themselves in a very difficult position, owing to the spirit of hostility against the Holy See, manifested by some of the bishops and representatives of the civil powers. At this session very little was accomplished. The formal opening of the council was announced, the date for the next public session was fixed, and safe conduct for the delegates of the Protestant princes was prepared.

Eighteenth Session (February 25, 1562). Besides the five legates, the Cardinal of Trent, three patriarchs, sixteen archbishops, one hundred and five bishops, five generals of religious orders and four abbots were present. Despite the earnest efforts of the legates it was found impossible to make any progress. Grave differences of opinion manifested themselves both within and without the council. The question whether bishops are bound to reside in their dioceses by divine or ecclesiastical law gave rise to prolonged and angry debates. Moreover, Spain demanded that a definite statement should be made to the effect that the council was only the continuation of the Council of Trent, while France insisted that it should be regarded as a distinct and independent council.

Nineteenth Session (May 14, 1562). Besides the five legates, this session was attended by one cardinal, three patriarchs, eighteen archbishops, one hundred and thirty-one bishops, four generals of religious orders and two abbots. No decree of any importance was passed.

Twentieth Session (June 4, 1562). At this session were present the five legates, one cardinal, two patriarchs, eighteen archbishops, one hundred and thirty-seven bishops, four generals of religious orders and two abbots. Various subjects were discussed, and the date for the next session was fixed.

Twenty-first Session (July 16, 1562). In this session the decrees on *Holy Communion* were passed. It was defined that there was "no divine law obliging the laity to receive Holy Communion under both kinds." "Sancta ipsa Synodus . . . declarat ac docet, nullo divino praecepto laicos et clericos non conficientes obligari ad Eucharistiae sacramentum sub utraque specie sumendum" (Chap. 1); "that Christ is really present whole and entire both under the appearance of bread and under the appearance of wine"— "declarat fatendum esse, etiam sub altera tantum specie totum atque integrum Christum verumque sacramentum sumi" (Chap. 3); "that infants who have not come to the use of reason, are not bound to receive Holy Communion, since they have been regenerated by baptism, and cannot lose, at that age, being already incorporated in Christ, the grace of adoption of the children of God"—"Eadem sancta Synodus docet, parvulos usu rationis carentes, nulla obligari necessitate ad sacramentalem Eucharistiae communionem, siquidem per Baptismi lavacrum regenerati et in Christo incorporati adeptam jam filiorum Dei gratiam in illa aetate amittere non possunt" (Chap. 4).

At this session were present the five legates, one cardinal, three patriarchs, nineteen archbishops, one hundred and forty-eight bishops, six generals of religious orders and four abbots.

Twenty-second Session (September 17, 1562). In this session nine chapters and nine canons on the *"Holy Sacrifice of the Mass"* were published. It was laid down "that in place of the sacrifices and the priesthood of the Old Law, Christ set up a new sacrifice, namely, the Mass, the clean oblation foretold by the Prophet Malachy, and a new priesthood, to whom he committed the celebration of Mass; that the sacrifice of the Mass is the same sacrifice as that of the Cross, having the same High-Priest and the same Victim, and that the Mass may be offered up for the living and for the dead." "Si quis dixerit, in Missa non offerri Deo verum et proprium sacrificium, aut quod off erri non sit aliud quam nobis Christum ad manducandum dari, anathema sit" (Canon 1). "Si quis dixerit, illis verbis: 'Hoc facite in meam commemorationem' Christum non instituisse Apostolos sacerdotes, aut non ordinasse, Ut ipsi aliique sacerdotes offerrent corpus et sanguinem, anathema sit" (Canon 2). "Quare non solum pro vivorum fidelium peccatis, satisfactionibus et aliis necessitatibus, sed et pro defunctis in Christo, nondum ad plenum purgatis, rite juxta Apostolorum traditionem offertur" (Chapter 4).

The question of allowing the laity to receive Holy Communion under both species was discussed at length, and it was finally decided to submit the question to the Pope. Pope Pius IV did, indeed, make a concession on this point in favor of several districts in Austria, but as the Catholics did not desire such a concession, and since the Lutherans refused to accept it as insufficient, the indult remained practically a dead-letter; later on it was entirely withdrawn.

The reform decree dealt with the life of the clergy. Present at this session were one hundred and eighty-two voters.

The next session was fixed for November 1562, but on account of very grave difficulties which arose, a much more prolonged adjournment was rendered necessary. During this interval the old controversies broke out with renewed violence and bitterness, and more than once, it appeared as if the council would break up in disorder but the perseverance, tact and energy of the new legates, Cardinals Morone and Navagero, who had been nominated after the death of the two Cardinals Gonzaga and Seripando, averted the threatened rupture, and made it possible for the fathers to accomplish the work for which they had been convoked. The question whether the residence of the bishops in their dioceses was obligatory by divine or ecclesiastical law, became very acute. Emperor Ferdinand I put forward a very comprehensive scheme of reform. Some of its portions were considered by the legates to be prejudicial to the rights of the Holy See, and were, therefore, rejected by them. Ferdinand asserted that there was no liberty at the council, and that it was entirely controlled by Rome. At his request several bishops left Trent, and joined Ferdinand at Innsbruck, where a kind of opposition assembly was begun. Cardinal Morone, realizing fully the seriousness of the situation, went to Innsbruck, where he had a personal interview with the Emperor in April 1563. The meeting resulted in clearing away many of the misunderstandings, which had arisen, and in bringing about a compromise.

Twenty-third Session (July 15, 1563). In this session it was defined that Christ instituted the Sacrament of *"Holy Orders";* that there are seven orders in the Church, two of which are expressly mentioned in Holy Scripture—priesthood and diaconate—(Acts, 6:5): "Ab ipso Ecclesiae initio sequentium ordinum nomina atque uniuscujusque eorum propria ministeria, subdiaconi scilicet, acolythi, exorcistae, lectoris et ostiarii in usu fuisse cognoscuntur" (Chapter 2); "Si quis dixerit praeter sacerdotium non esse in Ecclesia catholica alios ordines, et majores et minores, per quos velut per gradus quosdam in sacerdotium tendatur, anathema sit" (Canon 2); that there is a hierarchy in the Catholic Church, by divine ordination, consisting of bishops, priests and ministers "Si quis dixerit, in Ecclesia Catholica non esse hierarchiam, divina ordinatione institutam, quae constat ex episcopis, presbyteris et ministries anathema sit" (Canon 6); that the bishops are superior to the priests, that neither the consent of the people nor of the civil power is necessary for the valid reception of the orders "Si quis dixerit, episcopos non esse presbyteris superiores, vel non habere potestatern confirmandi et ordinandi, vel eam, quam habent, illis esse communem cum presbyteris; vel ordines ab ipsis collatos sine populi vel potestatis saecularis consensu aut vocatione irritos esse; aut eos, qui nec ab ecclesiastica et canonica potestate rite ordinati nec missi sunt, sed aliunde veniunt, legitimos esse verbi et sacramentorum ministros: anathema sit" (Canon 7); and that the bishops who are appointed by the authority of the Roman Pontiff, are true bishops: "Si quis dixerit, episcopos, qui auctoritate Romani Pontificis assumuntur, non esse legitimos et veros episcopos, sed figmentum humanum, anathema sit" (Canon 8).

The question whether the duty of episcopal residence is of divine law, about which such a protracted and heated controversy had been waged, was settled amicably by deciding that the bishops as pastors are bound by divine command to know their flocks, and that they cannot acquire this knowledge unless they reside in their dioceses. This was the subject of the reform decree.

At this session there were present four cardinals, three patriarchs, twenty-five archbishops, one hundred and ninety-three bishops, four generals of religious orders and three abbots.

Twenty-fourth Session (November 11, 1563). The decrees on the nature and sacramental character of *"Matrimony"* were published. The council defined that matrimony is truly one of the seven sacraments of the evangelical law, instituted by Christ; that Christians may not have several wives simultaneously; that the Church has the power to establish diriment impediments; that adultery does not dissolve the bond of matrimony; that clerics in sacred orders and religious who have made the solemn vow of chastity cannot contract matrimony validly. "Si quis dixerit, matrimonium non esse vere et proprie unum ex septem Legis evangelicae sacramentis, a Christo Domino institutum, sed ab hominibus in Ecclesia inventum, neque gratiam conferre: anathema sit" (Canon 1). "Si quis dixerit, licere Christianis plures simul habere uxores, et hoc nulla lege divina esse prohibitum: anathema sit" (Canon 2). "Si quis dixerit, Ecclesiam non potuisse constituere impedimenta matrimoniorum dirimentia, vel in us constituendis errasse: anathema sit" (Canon 4). "Si quis dixerit, Ecclesiam errare, cum docuit et docet, juxta evangelicam et apostolicam doctrinam, propter adulterium alterius conjugum matrimonii vinculum non posse dissolvi...anathema sit" (Canon 7). "Si quis dixerit, clericos in sacris ordinibus constitutos, vel regulares castitatem solemniter professos, posse matrimonium contrahere, contractumque validum esse...anathema sit" (Canon 9).

The reform decrees, promulgated in this session, forbid by the famous decree *"Tametsi dubitandum non est"* (Though there is no doubt) *clandestine marriages:* "Qui aliter quam praeserite parocho, vel alio sacerdote de ipsius parochi seu Ordinarii licentia, et duobus vel tribus testibus matrimonium contrahere attentabunt, eos sancta Synodus ad sic contrahendum omnino inhabiles reddit, et hujusmodi contractu irritos et nullos esse decernit." "Those who shall attempt to contract marriage otherwise than in the presence of the Pastor, or another Priest with the permission of the Pastor or Ordinary, and in the presence of two or three witnesses, this holy Synod makes them entirely unfit to enter upon such a marriage, and declares such contracts null and void" (Chapter 1). The council also renewed the ancient prohibitions of solemn nuptials from Advent to Epiphany and from Ash Wednesday until the Octave of Easter (Canon 11). The other disciplinary decrees speak of the procedure to be followed in the election of bishops and cardinals; of the holding of provincial synods every third year, and of Diocesan synods every year.

All were anxious to bring the council to an end. In accordance with the general desire the addresses were cut short, and so rapid was the progress that the last session could be announced for December.

Twenty-fifth Session (December 3 and 4, 1563). The decrees on *"Purgatory, Veneration of the Saints and their Relics,"* and on *"Indulgences"* were promulgated. "Cum catholica Ecclesia...et in hac oecumenica Synodo docuerit, purgatorium esse, animasque ibi detentas fidelium suffragiis, potissimum vero acceptabili altaris sacrificio juvari praecipit sancta Synodus episcopis, ut sanam doctrinam de purgatorio, a sanctis Patribus et sacris Conciliis traditam, a Christifidelibus credi, teneri, doceri et ubique praedicari studeant." "Since the Catholic Church... and lately in this Ecumenical Synod has taught that there is a purgatory, and that the souls detained there are assisted by the suffrages of the faithful, especially by the acceptable sacrifice of Mass the holy Synod enjoins on the Bishops to take pains that the wise doctrine of purgatory, handed down by the Holy Fathers and holy Synods is believed, held by the faithful of Christ, and taught and preached everywhere." The council renews the teaching of the Second Ecumenical Council of Nicaea held in 787, concerning the veneration of the saints and their relics.

Concerning indulgences the Holy Synod decreed: "Sacrosancta Synodus indulgentiarum usum, christiano populo maxime salutarem et sacrorum Conciliorum auctoritate probatum, in Ecclesia retinendum esse docet et praecipit, eosque anathemate damnat, qui aut inutiles esse asserunt, vel eas concedendi in Ecclesia potestatem esse negant." "The holy Synod teaches and commands that the use of indulgences, so very salutary to the Christian people and sanctioned by holy Councils, must be retained in the Church, and pronounces anathema over those who assert that they are useless or deny the power of the Church to grant them" (Decree on Indulgences).

The reform decrees treated of fast days and holy days, in the observance of which the custom of the Roman Church should be followed; of monastic life; of the relation of the regular clergy to the bishop; of forbidden books and of a revision and new edition of the missal and breviary. Thereupon the decrees which had been passed in the First Period under Paul III and in the Second Period under Julius III were read and accepted. The legates were asked to obtain the approval of the Pope for the decisions of the council.

Cardinal Morone, the first Legate and President of the Council then blessed the assembled prelates, and after the singing of the *Te Deum*, he dismissed them with the customary formula: "Most Reverend Fathers, go in peace." And all answered with heart and mind "Amen." Tears flowed from the eyes of every one of the Fathers, with mutual embraces, congratulated each other upon the successful outcome of their work. Finally, all signed their names to the acts of the council, namely, four cardinal-legates, two cardinals, three patriarchs, twenty-five archbishops, one hundred and sixty-seven bishops, seven generals of religious orders, seven abbots, and nineteen procurators in the name of thirty-three absent prelates.

On the conclusion of the council, Cardinal Morone hastened to Rome to seek the approval of the Pope for the decrees. On January 26, 1564 Pope Pius IV issued the bull of confirmation, saying that the decrees would go into effect on May 1, 1564.

Italy received the decrees of the council immediately so also King Sebastian of Portugal. Philip II, King of Spain, acted similarly, except that he insisted on the addition of a saving clause: "without prejudice to royal authority." Emperor Ferdinand I hesitated for some time to accept the decrees, but finally gave in (1566). In France, the dogmatic decrees were accepted; but as several reform decrees, notably those relating to marriage, benefices, etc., were opposed to the civil law, permission to publish them was refused. However, the reform decrees were gradually promulgated in the provincial synods.

A *"Profession of Faith,"* based on the decrees of the Council of Trent, was drawn up by Pius IV on November 13, 1564. This profession of faith had to be made by those who were appointed to ecclesiastical dignities, who received an academic degree, and who were converts from Protestantism.

The *"Catechism of the Council of Trent"* was prepared by St. Pius V, a Dominican, and published in 1566. It is a most valuable work of instruction, approved by the highest authority in the Church.

The Council of Trent met under very difficult conditions and circumstances, and it carried on its work in face of great opposition and disappointments. More than once it was interrupted for a long period, and more than once, too, it was feared by many that it would result in creating schism rather than in promoting unity. But under the Providence of God the dangers were averted, the arms of the enemies were weakened, and the hearts of the faithful children of the Church throughout the world were filled with joy and gratitude. Never had a council of the Church met under more alarming conditions; never had a council been confronted with more serious obstacles, and never did a council confer a greater service on the Christian world than did the Council of Trent from 1545 to 1563.

XX
THE TWENTIETH ECUMENICAL COUNCIL
HELD AT THE VATICAN, ROME, 1869–1870

WORK OF THE COUNCIL: Condemnation of existing errors and definition of papal infallibility.

More than three hundred years had elapsed since the celebration of the Council of Trent. We do not meet another period in the history of the Church so long without the convocation of an ecumenical council. To counteract the prevalent machinations which threatened to overthrow the supernatural order, Pius IX, on December 6, 1864, communicated to certain cardinals, under the seal of secrecy, his intention of convoking an ecumenical council, and requested the cardinals then present in Rome to furnish him a statement of their views. Nearly all of them were in favor of holding a council. In March 1865, Pius IX appointed a central commission of five cardinals (Patrizzi, Reisach, Panebianco, Bizzari, Caterini) to report on the advisability of a council. In April and May 1865, letters were sent to thirty-six of the leading bishops of the Latin Rite, and, later on, to the principal bishops of the Oriental Rite concerning the advisability of holding a synod. The replies of the bishops were favorable to the idea.

In 1867, Pope Pius IX invited the bishops of the world to attend the celebration of the eighteenth centenary of the martyrdom of St. Peter and St. Paul in Rome. Great numbers from all parts of the world attended, and in a public consistory, held on June 26, 1867, the Pope announced his intention of holding an ecumenical council. The bishops, in their reply on July 2, 1867, congratulated the Pope on his resolve and promised him their earnest co-operation. The central commission advised that five auxiliary commissions should be established: one for doctrine, one for ecclesiastico-political questions, one for missions and the reunion of the Churches, one for discipline, and one for religious orders; and that in addition to the Roman theologians and canonists, distinguished scholars should be invited from all parts of the world to attend the council (August 11, 1867). This suggestion was accepted and Church historians of repute and theologians were called to Rome. Hefele, Schraeder, Hergenroether, Alzog, Hettinger were among the distinguished representatives of Germany; Feye represented Louvain; Gay, Freppel, Gibert, Chesnel were among the French scholars; Canon Weathers, Rector of St. Edmund's, attended from England, and Dr. Corcoran of Charleston from the United States of America.

The bull *Aeterni Patris* (Of the Eternal Father), which was based on the bull of Paul III, convoking the Council of Trent in 1542, was issued by Pius IX on June 29, 1868, convoking the Vatican Council, to open on December 8, 1869.

On September 8, 1868, Pius IX invited the Eastern bishops, not in communion with Rome, to the coming council. On September 13, 1868, he sent an invitation to the Protestants to return to Catholic unity. Both these parties declined to take part in the council.

The convocation of the council, while pleasing to the vast body of the Catholic clergy and people, roused the bitter enmity of the radical-liberal party throughout Europe. Even in Catholic circles bitter controversies broke out, especially in Germany and France. The ablest opponent in Germany at this period was Doctor Ignatius von Doellinger, Professor of Church History at the University of Munich. As an historian, Doellinger stood in the front rank of his profession, and, as a writer and speaker, he had wrought wonders for the Catholic Church in Germany; but as his reputation for learning became greater, his respect for the Church and Church authority grew less. The knowledge that he was distrusted in Rome embittered his feelings, so that from 1867 on it was well known that Doellinger must be reckoned among the strong opponents of the council. In 1868 he contributed a series of letters, principally on the question of papal infallibility, to an Augsburg paper. These at once attracted general attention on account of the bitterness with which he discussed the question. In 1869 Doellinger published the book *Janus*, a summary of all the historical objections which could be urged against papal infallibility. Refutations of this book were not few. The best of these was undoubtedly *The Anti-Janus*, written by Professor Hergenroether of Wuerzburg, an able historian, who knew how to combine scientific investigation with due respect for the divinely constituted authority of the Church.

In France, the most active opponent of papal infallibility was Bishop Dupanloup of Orleans, who was supported by Cardinal Mathieu of Besançon, by Archbishop Darboy of Paris, and by Bishop Maret, Dean of the Theological Faculty of the Sorbonne, and by other lesser personages.

In Belgium, the feeling was general in favor of papal infallibility. Archbishop Deschamps of Malines was its prominent supporter, and in his efforts he was seconded by the professors of Louvain University.

In England, Cardinal Manning was recognized as a leader in the movement for the definition of papal infallibility, and he was ably helped by Monsignor Ward in the *Dublin Review*. In Ireland Dr. Murray was a strong supporter of papal infallibility.

In the United States of America, the principal opponent to the definition of papal infallibility was the Most Reverend Peter Richard Kenrick, Archbishop of St. Louis, Missouri.

While the controversies were going on in almost every country of the world, the central commission was at work in Rome preparing the general direction of the council and special commissions were engaged in drafting the schemata, which were to be submitted to the fathers. Four committees were selected, each consisting of twenty-four members, to deal with the four classes of subjects: faith, discipline, Oriental Church, and religious orders. Each committee was directed to discuss the schema and then submit it to the general congregation of the council for discussion. If, after due discussion, the schema was accepted, a public session of the council could be held at once in the presence of the Pope and then the decrees could be promulgated. If, however, serious changes had to be made, or if the schema was rejected entirely, the committee had to submit it again in an improved form.

Proceedings of the Council

Opening of the Council. Pope Pius IX opened the council with great solemnity in St. Peter's on December 8, 1869. The customary prayers were said, and the Archbishop of Iconium, Passavalli, O.M. Cap., preached the sermon on this occasion.

First Session (December 8, 1869). The council was declared officially opened, and the next session was announced for January 6, 1870. The number of the participants in the Vatican Council varied at different times. The highest number present at any time was 774: forty-nine cardinals, ten patriarchs, ten primates, one hundred and twenty-seven archbishops, five hundred and twenty-nine bishops, twenty-two abbots, twenty-six generals of religious orders, and one apostolic administrator. The total number of those who were entitled to be present was about 1,050, so that about 280 were absent through age, sickness, or for some other good reason. If the Vatican Council be viewed from the point of number of bishops present, it is the largest and most representative council held in the history of the Church.

On the same day, December 8, 1869, the "Brothers of the Three Points" (Freemasons) opened a grand council of their infamous order in Naples. This gathering had been decreed at a Masonic banquet given in Paris on the Good Friday previous for the express purpose of manifesting a diabolical hatred of the God-Man. At this banquet to the accompaniment of blasphemies "sausages were flung at the Head of Christ, and the representation of Calvary was smeared with scraps of pork" (Rivaux, Eccles. Hist. Vol. III, page 60).

The General Congregations opened their sessions on December 10, 1869. Before January 6, 1870 they held seven general meetings.

Second Session (January 6, 1870). Because no schema was so far advanced in its preparation as to be proposed to the fathers of the council for voting, all present made the customary profession of faith.

Between this and the next session twenty-two general meetings were held.

Though the question of papal infallibility was not yet on the schemata to be submitted to the council, the controversies of the previous year had brought it into such considerable prominence that from the very beginning of the council the friends and the opponents of the definition were not idle. In December 1869, Archbishop Deschamps sent a request to the congregations appointed to deal with such proposals that the question of papal infallibility should be defined by the council. About the same time the leading supporters of infallibility (Manning of England, Martin of Paderborn, von Senestrey of Ratisbon, Spalding of Baltimore, and others), agreed that a petition which would demand the definition of the dogma should be prepared and circulated in order to obtain the signatures of the fathers. It was signed by 380, and about 100 bishops signed other petitions of a similar kind, so that altogether about 480 of the fathers requested that the question of papal infallibility should be placed upon the schemata. On the other hand, the opponents of infallibility were not idle. Cardinal Schwarzenberg of Prague, Cardinal Rauscher of Vienna, Strossmayer of Diakovar, Darboy of Paris, and Dupanloup of Orleans were particularly active. Instead of one common petition against infallibility, five separate ones were handed in. The first of these from the German, Austrian and Hungarian bishops bore the signatures of sixty-four bishops; the second, mainly from the French and Portuguese, was signed by forty bishops; the third, from the Italians, was subscribed to by seven bishops; the fourth, mainly from the North Americans, England and Ireland, had the signatures of twenty-three bishops; the fifth, from the Orientals, was signed by sixteen bishops. American bishops against infallibility were Archbishop Kenrick of St. Louis, Archbishop Purcell of Cincinnati, Bishop Berot of Savannah, Bishop Domenec of Pittsburg, Bishop McQuaid of Rochester, Bishop Mrak of Marquette, Bishop Fitzgerald of Little Rock and Bishop Connelly of Halifax. The two Irish bishops who signed the counter petition were Moriarty of Kerry and Leahy of Dromore, while the two English bishops who had affixed their signatures were Errington, the former Coadjutor of Westminster, and Clifford of Clifton. The two petitions—pro and con—were considered by the congregation charged with the examination of such proposals on February 9, 1870. With the exception of Cardinal Rauscher of Vienna, all the members of the congregation voted in favor of including papal infallibility in the program of the council. Pius IX approved of their decision.

The excitement both within and without the council became greater every day. The greater part of the German and Austrian bishops were opposed to the definition, but their opposition was based principally on the danger which would result from such a definition in Germany rather than on objections to the doctrine itself. About one-third of the episcopate of France was in the ranks of the opposition, but they too professed that they opposed the definition not from the doctrinal standpoint but for reasons of prudence. Archbishop Darboy of Paris and Bishop Dupanloup of Orleans seem to have spared no pains to secure a victory for their views. In Germany Doellinger carried on his unbridled campaign. From December 16, 1869 till July 19, 1870 a series of sixty-nine articles, entitled *Roemische Briefe* (Roman letters) appeared in the Augsburg Ailgemeine Zeitung. Doellinger had probably a great share in the composition of these letters, but the information was supplied mainly by Friederich, the theologian of Cardinal Hohenlohe, and by Sir John Acton (Granderath, Gesch. des Vat. Konzils, Vol. III, 599–602).

Very able replies to these letters were issued by Hergenroether, Scheeben, Stoekl and Zahn. The bishops of Germany publicly disassociated themselves from the Doellinger campaign.

In the meantime the schema *On Faith* had been so thoroughly debated and recast that it was ready for final voting and promulgation.

Third Session (April 24, 1870). The schema On Faith was accepted and promulgated by Pius IX in the constitution *Dei Filius* (The Son of God). This constitution condemns atheism, pantheism, materialism, the errors of Guenther and Hermes, the errors of the pseudo-philosophers and pseudo-theologians; it defines the necessity of revelation, and emphasizes the necessity of faith, the impossibility of opposition between faith and reason and the mutual aid which faith and science render to each other. This constitution contained five canons on God the Creator of all things; four canons on Revelation; six canons on Faith, and three canons on Faith and Reason.

Six hundred and sixty-seven voters were present at this session.

The majority of the bishops were of the opinion that because of the excitement which raged around the definition of papal infallibility, the question should be determined immediately. On April 27, 1870, the Cardinal Prefect announced that the schema *"On the Roman Pontiff"* should be taken up. On April 29th, seventy-one bishops signed a protest against it and demanded that this protest should be presented to the Holy Father. The Committee "On Faith" proceeded to draft the formal decrees. There was great difficulty in presenting an acceptable formula for the definition of papal infallibility. Cardinal Bilio suggested that the formula should state that the Pope was infallible whenever, as Supreme Pastor, he taught that something should be accepted by the whole Church as of "divine Faith," or that something should be rejected as opposed to "divine Faith." This formula was agreeable to most of the bishops, except to Manning and von Senestrey.

On May 13th the general debate began in the council. It lasted till June 13th, during which time fourteen general meetings were held and sixty-four speeches were made by bishops from all parts of the world. On June 13th, Cardinal de Angelis with a vast majority were in favor of closing the general debate. A protest was lodged against this proceeding by Cardinals Mathieu, Schwarzenberg and Rauscher in the name of eighty-one bishops.

The difficulty of agreeing on a suitable formula for the definition of papal infallibility still continued. At last on June 18, Dr. Cullen of Dublin proposed a formula which with a few slight changes gave general satisfaction. The public session for the solemn ratification of the decree was fixed for July 18, 1870.

During the intervening days the minority made great efforts to secure the insertion of their amendments in the text, or to have the solemn definition of the doctrine postponed. To obtain either the one or the other of their demands, six of their number, Darboy (Paris), Cinoulhiac (Lyons), Simor (Gran), Scherr (Munich), Ketteler (Mayence), and Rivot (Dijon) went as a deputation to Pius IX, but the Pope declined to interfere with the decisions of the council. The minority were, therefore, obliged to make up their minds, either to attend the public session, and vote against the definition, or to take their departure from Rome before the session for the definition would be held.

Fourth Session (July 18, 1870). In this session the *"Dogmatic Constitution on the Church of Christ"*—*"Pastor aeternus"* (Eternal Pastor) was accepted. The constitution treats of the institution of the primacy in Blessed Peter, of the perpetuity of the primacy of Blessed Peter in the Roman Pontiffs, of the rights and the significance of the primacy of the Roman Pontiff, of the infallible teaching authority of the Roman Pontiff, in which section the constitution cites the Fourth Ecumenical Council of Constantinople (870), the Second Ecumenical Council of Lyons (1274) and the Ecumenical Council of Florence (1445), and the Constitution concludes with the *Definition of Infallibility:* "Itaque Nos traditioni a fidei christianae exordio perceptae fideliter inhaerendo, ad Dei Salvatoris nostri gloriam, religionis catholicae exaltationem et christianorum populorum salutem, sacro approbante Concilio, docemus et divinitus revelatum dogma esse definimus: Romanum Pontificem, cum ex cathedra loquitur, id est, cum omnium Christianorum pastoris et doctoris munere fungens pro suprema sua Apostolica auctoritate doctrinam de fide vel moribus ab universa Ecclesia tenendam definit, per assistentiam divinam ipsi in beato Petro promissam, ea infallibilitate pollere, qua divinus Redemptor Ecclesiam suam in definienda doctrina de fide vel moribus instructam esse voluit; ideoque ejusmodi Romani Pontificis definitiones ex sese, non autem ex consensu Ecclesiae, irreformabiles esse." Canon: "Si quis autem huic Nostrae definitioni contradicere, quod Deus avertat, praesumpserit, anathema sit." "We, therefore, adhering to the tradition perceived from the beginning of the Christian Faith, for the glory of our God-Saviour, for the exaltation of the Catholic religion and for the salvation of Christian peoples, with the approval of the Holy Council, teach and define that it is a dogma divinely revealed: That the Roman Pontiff, when he speaks ex cathedra, that is, when in the discharge of his office as pastor and teacher of all Christians, by virtue of his supreme apostolic authority, he defines a doctrine regarding faith or morals, to be held by the Universal Church, is by divine assistance promised to him in Blessed Peter, possessed of that infallibility with which the Divine Redeemer willed that the Church should be endowed in defining doctrine regarding faith or morals; and that, therefore, such definitions of the Roman Pontiffs are of themselves, and not from the consent of the Church, irreformable." *Canon:* "If any one should presume to contradict this our definition, which God avert, let him be anathema."

Of the bishops present, five hundred and thirty-three voted in the affirmative, and only two in the negative, namely, Bishop Riccio of Cajazzo in Sicily, and Bishop Fitzgerald of Little Rock, Arkansas. Some bishops from Germany, Austria, Hungary, and United States of America, fifty-five in all, absented themselves from this solemn session. Pope Pius IX, amid lightning and thunder, promulgated the decree of the council, and the two bishops who had voted against the definition made their humble submission immediately after the publication of the decree. These two bishops who voted negatively rendered great service to the council inasmuch as they proved conclusively that the council was absolutely free in its action.

War was declared between France and Germany on July 19, 1870, and most of the bishops left Rome. It was well known that an invasion of the city of Rome might be expected immediately. The debate on the schema of discipline was begun, but it was not concluded when the city was surrounded by the forces of Italy. On October 20, 1870, Pius IX issued a decree, proroguing the council. Some of the bishops, notably Manning, Cullen and Spalding (Baltimore) were anxious for the council to continue its work in Malines, but their plan did not find support.

The Vatican Council was convoked as a remedy for the evils of the time; its object was to unmask the enemy of Christian society. In proclaiming the *Infallibility of the Pope,* this august assembly gave to the world a principle which regenerates authority; one, which in the course of time, will re-establish in society—order, peace and unity.

"Jesus Christ has three existences: His personal existence, which Arius denied; His sacramental existence, which Calvin denied, and that other existence which completes the two, and by means of which He continually lives, through His authority, in the person of His Vicar. The Council of the Vatican, in proclaiming this third existence, has completed the task of assuring the world of the possession of Jesus Christ."

BIBLIOGRAPHY

Alzog, Universal Church History
Bruek, History of the Catholic Church
Bullarium Romanum
Butler, The Vatican Council (2 vols.)
Catholic Encyclopedia
Denzinger, Enchiridion Symbolorum et Definitionum
Hefele, Conciliengeschichte
Herder's Konversationslexikon
Hergenroether, Handbuch der ailgemeinen Kirchen Geschichte
Holzapfel, Historia Ordinis Fratrum Minorum
Koch, Jesuiten-Lexikon
Guilday, Church Historians
Gilmartin, Manual of Church History
Knöpfler, Manual of Church History
Manning, The Vatican Council
Mansi, Sacrorum Conciliorum Nova et Amplissima Collectio
Muller, Das Konzil von Vienne
Parsons, Studies in Church History
Pastor, History of the Popes
Ritter, Handbuch der Kirchengeschichte
Universal Knowledge, Encyclopedia of
Vaticanum im Lichte des katholischen Glaubens
Wetzer und Welte, Kirchenlexikon
Pallavicini, Geschichte des Trienter Concils
Grisar, Analecta Romana, Geschichte Roms im Mittelalter
Hurter, Pontifikat Innocenz III
Hettinger, Apologie des Christentums
Granderath, Geschichte des Vatikanischen Konzils

INDEX

Abundantius of Paterno, papal legate to 6th Ecum. Council, 24.
Ad providam, bull of Clement V, disposing of property of Knights Templars, 63.
Aeterni Patris, bull of Pius IX, convoking Vatican Council, 108.
Aeternus Pastor, dogmatic constitution of Pius IX, 113.
Agatho, St., I, Pope; orders synods to condemn Monothelitism, 24. sends Dogmatic Epistle to 6th Ecum. Council, 24; defends Pope Honorius I, 27.
Albergati, Cardinal, President of Union Council at Ferrara, 78.
Albigensian heresy, condemnation of, 46, 49.
Alexander III, Pope: eulogized by Voltaire, 44; triumphs over Frederick Barbarossa, 44; convokes 11th Ecum. Council, 45.
Alexander, Bishop of Alexandria, contradicted by Arius, 2, 3.
Alexandria: St. Peter bishop of, excommunicates Meletians, 2; synod of, condemns heresy of Arius, 2; St. Cyril of, at 3rd Ecum. Council, 9.
Anacletus II, anti-pope: aided by Roger of Sicily, 41; his ordinations declared null, 42.
Ancyra, 31, 35.
Anatolius, Patriarch of Constantinople: asks for confirmation of the Council of Chalcedon, 17; is rebuked by Leo I, 17.
Anathemas of St. Cyril, 9; counter, of Nestorius, 9; condemning "Three Chapters," 21.
Andrew, King of Hungary, and Crusade, 52.
Anthony Messanus, Franciscan, and union with Greek Church, 78.
Anti-Janus, by Hergenroether, 109.
Apamea, Constantine, teaches existence of two wills in Christ, 26.
Apostolical Council, decrees of, 1.
Apostolici Regiminis, bull of Leo X, 88.
Aquileia, breaks off Communion with Holy See, 21.
Aquinas, St. Thomas, called to 14th Ecum. Council, 56.
Arcadius, papal legate to 3rd Ecum. Council at Ephesus, 10.
Arius: arch-heretic, author of Arianism, 2; his errors, 2; his condemnation, 3.

Armenians, return to Roman Church at 17th Ecum. Council, 83.
Asbestas, Gregory, Bishop of Syracuse: ordained Photius, 33; favored Photian schism, 33; suspended by Nicholas I, 34 excommunicated by 8th Ecum. Council, 36.
Ascoli, Jerome of, Franciscan, and Greek Union, 55.
Assisi, St. Francis of, at 4th Lateran Council, 50.
Athanasian Creed, 8.
Athanasius, St., at 1st Ecum. Council, 2.
Augsburg, adherents of Confession of, 100.

Baptism, Sacrament of, discussion at Council of Trent, 95.
Barbarossa, Frederick: peace with Alexander III, 44; vow to start on Crusade, 5; excommunicated at 13th Ecum. Council, 54.
Bardas, opponent of Ignatius of Constantinople, 33.
Basil, St., refutes Macedonianism, 5.
Basil, Emperor: expels Photius, 34 recalls Ignatius from exile, 34 notification to Pope Nicholas I, 34.
Basilius, Bishop of Ancyra, abjures iconoclasm, 31.
Basilius, papal legate to 4th Ecum. Council at Chalcedon, 15.
Basel, 17th Ecum. Council (1435): 73; hostile measures of council against Papacy, 74, 74, 75 dissolved by Eugene IV, 77 stubbornly continues, 77; ecumenical character of, 77.
Bassian, Bishop of Ephesus, case examined by 4th Ecum. Council at Chalcedon, 17.
Benedict XIII, anti-pope: his adherents, 66; his stubbornness, 69; deposed by 16th Ecum. Council of Constance, 70.
Berengarius, Raymond, Franciscan, and Greek Union, 55.
Beser, defender of iconoclasm, 29.
Bologna, Council of Trent transferred to, 95.
Bonagratia, Franciscan, and Greek Union, 55.
Bonaventure, Franciscan sent by Gregory X to work for Greek Union, 55.
Bonaventure, St., created cardinal by Gregory X, 56; at 14th Ecum. Council, 56.

Boniface, papal legate to 4th Ecum. Council, 15.

Books, printing of, regulated by 8th Ecum. Council, 89.

Bourges, Pragmatic Sanction of: issued by Charles VII, 87, abrogated at 18th Ecum. Council, 87.

Bruys, Peter of, condemnation of his heresy, 42.

Bulls: *Ad providam* of Clement V, disposing of the property of the Knights Templars, 63; *Aeterni patris* of Pius IX, convoking the Vatican Council, 108, *Exivi de paradiso* of Clement V, explaining Rule of Franciscan Order, 63, *Laetare Jerusalem* of Paul III, opening Council of Trent, 93, *Vineam Domini* of Innocent III, convoking 12th Ecum. Council, 48, *Vox in excelso* of Clement V, suppressing Knights Templars, 62.

Caerularius, Michael, break with Rome (1054), 36.

Calendar, reform of, 89.

Callistus II, Pope, settles investiture at Diet of Worms, 39.

Canonical Scriptures, decree of Council of Trent, 94.

Canons: Council of Nicaea, 4 Council of Constantinople, 7 Council of Ephesus, 11; Council of Chalcedon, 17, Council of Nicaea, 32; Council of Constantinople, 36; Council of the Lateran, 39, Council of the Lateran, 43, Council of the Lateran, 46 Council of the Lateran, 49 Council of Lyons, 54, Council of Lyons, 58, 59; Council of Vienne, 63, Council of Constance, 72.

Cardinals: tenth part of revenue to Crusades, 49, 56; refractory, convoked Council of Pisa in 1511, 85; central commission of, to report on advisability of holding Ecum. Council of Vatican, 108.

Carraffa, Peter Cardinal, Pope Paul IV, 100.

Catechism of Council of Trent, 106.

Celestine, I, St.: writes to St. Cyril of Alexandria and Nestorius, 9; sends legates to Council of Ephesus, 10; confirms Council of Ephesus, 12.

Cervini, Marcellus Cardinal, appointed president of Council of Trent, 92.

Cerinthians, heresy of, 8.

Cesarini, Cardinal: legate of Holy See for Crusade against Hussites, 73; president of Council of Basel, 73.

Chalcedon, 4th Ecum. Council at (451): 13; condemns heresy of Eutyches, 13; issued thirty canons, 17; papal legates protest against 28th canon, 17; *Dogmatic Epistle* of Pope Leo I, 14; profession of Faith, 16; confirmation of council by Leo I, 17.

Chalice, lay, Communion both species discussion at Council of Trent, 102.

Chapters, Three, condemned at 5th Ecum. Council at Constantinople, 20, 21.

Charles Borromeo, St., at Council of Trent, 101.

Charles V, Emperor, and Council of Trent, 92.

Christ: divinity of, 3; Mother of, 10.

Chrysologus, St. Peter, Eutyches appeals to, 13.

Chrysorrhoas, St. John (Damascene), writings against iconoclasm, 30.

Clandestine marriages, nullified by Council of Trent, 105.

Clement V, Pope: permanent residence in Avignon, 60; resistance to King Philip, 60; convokes 15th Ecum. Council, 61; and case of Knights Templars, 62; settles controversy regarding Franciscan vow of poverty, 63; issues bull *Exivi de paradiso* explaining Rule of Franciscan Order, 63; issues constitution *Fidei Catholicae fundamento*, 63.

Clerics, canon 26 of 11th Ecum. Council regarding, 46.

Colonna, Cardinal (Martin V), and Council of Constance, 70.

Communion: of infants, discussion at Council of Trent, 102; Pascal, and 12th Ecum. Council, 49.

Concordat of Worms, abolition of investiture, 39.

Condemnations: of Arius, 4, of Macedonius and Marathonius, 5; of Nestorius, 10; of Eutyches, 16; of the "Three Chapters," 21; of Monothelitism, 26, of iconoclasm, 29; of Photius, 35; of Peter of Bruys, 42; of Albigensian heresy, 50; of Frederick Barbarossa, 52; of Wyclif and John Huss, 71; of errors of innovators at Council of Trent, 91, of atheism, pantheism, materialism, and errors of

pseudo-philosophers and pseudo-theologians at Vatican Council, 112.
Confession of Augsburg, adherents of, 100.
Confession, yearly, ordained by 12th Ecum. Council, 49.
Confirmation, Sacrament of, discussion at Council of Trent, 95.
Constance, 16th Ecumenical Council of (1414): 65, authority of council over Pope, 68, condemns heresies of Wyclif and John Huss, 71; deposes John XXIII, 69; deposes Benedict XIII, 70; accepts resignation of Gregory XII, 69; elects Cardinal Colonna Pope Martin V, 70.
Constans II, Emperor, issues *Typus*, 24.
Constantine the Great, and Council of Nicaea, 2, 3, 4.
Constantine, papal legate to 6th Ecum. Council, 25.
Constantine Copronymus, Emperor, iconoclast, 30.
Constantine Pogonatus, Emperor: convokes 6th Ecum. Council at Constantinople, 25; writes to Pope Donus, 24.
Constantine Porphyrogenitus-Emperor, signs profession of Faith of Seventh Ecum. Council, 4.
Constantinople, Second Ecumenical Council at (381): 5; condemnation of the heresy of Macedonius and other work of, 6; canons issued by, 7; ecumenical only in dogmatical utterances, 30.
  5th Ecumenical Council at (553): 19; condemnation of "Three Chapters," 19, 21; Pope Vigilius issues *Judicatum* and *Constitutum*, 20; and second *Constitutum*, 21; gradual recognition of ecumenical character, 21.
  6th Ecumenical Council at (680): 23; Monothelitism, 23, 26; Emperor Heraclius issues *Ekthesis*, 24; Constantine Pogonatus asks for an Ecum. Council, 24; Pope Agatho sends legates and *Dogmatic Epistle*, 24; issues profession of Faith, 26; Monothelitism condemned, 26; Leo II confirms acts of council with correction, 27; word on Pope Honorius I, 5.
  8th Ecumenical Council at (869): purpose to combat Photian schism, 33; deposes Pope Nicholas in pseudo-synod, 34; Emperor Basil ousts Photius, 36; asks Pope Hadrian II for an Ecum. Council, 34; Pope sends legates, 35; "Document of Reconciliation," 35; Photius is deposed, 35.
  Synod of (754) endorses iconoclasm, 30.
  Synod of (861), 34.
Constitutions, Dogmatic: *Dei Filius* of Pius IX, condemning prevalent errors, 112; *Fidei Catholicae fundamento* of Clement V, condemning errors of Peter Olivi, 63; *Pastor aeternus* of Pius IX on the Church of Christ, 113.
Consubstantiality, touchstone of orthodoxy, 3; Council of Nicaea, 1.
Creed: Athanasian, 1; Nicene, 3; Nicene-Constantinopolitan, 7.
Crescenzi, Cardinal legate to Council of Trent, 97.
Crusades, aid for, 49, 56.
Cyril, St., Bishop of Alexandria, 9; combats Nestorian heresy, 31; reports to St. Celestine I, 9 anathemas against Nestorius, 9; champion of orthodoxy at Council of Ephesus, 10.

D'Allemand, Cardinal Louis, leader of fanatics at Council of Basel, 75.
Damascene, St. John, writings regarding veneration of saints, images and relics, 30.
Damasus, I, St., Pope, condemns Macedonianism, 5.
Darboy, Archbishop of Paris, opponent of papal infallibility, 112.
Definition, dogmatic, of Union Council of Florence, 81.
Dei Filius, dogmatic Constitution of Pius IX, 112.
Del Monte, John Maria Cardinal appointed president of Council of Trent, 92; later Pope Julius III, 96; and Council of Trent, 97.
Deschamps, Archbishop of Malines, and papal infallibility, 109.
Diet of Worms, 39.
Dioscorus, Bishop of Alexandria: presides at Robber Synod of Ephesus, 14; deposed by 4th Ecum. Council, 15.
Disputa, of Raphael, 98.
Divinity of Christ, defined by 1st Ecum. Council, 3.

Divinity of the Holy Ghost, defined by 2nd Ecum. Council, 6.
Doellinger, Ignatius von: enemy of Vatican Council, 109; *Janus*, summary of historical objections to papal infallibility, 109; *Roemische Briefe,* 111.
Dogmatic Epistles: of St. Agatho to 6th Ecum. Council, 24; of St. Leo to 4th Ecum. Council, 14, 16.
Dominici, John Cardinal, plenipotentiary of Gregory XII, 67.
Donatists, 1.
Dupanloup, Archbishop of Orleans, and papal infallibility, 109.

Easter, calculations for and celebration of, 4.
Ekthesis, of Heraclius, favoring Monothelitism, 24.
Election: of new Pope at Council of Constance, 70; decree on papal, issued by the 11th Ecum. Council, 45, 58.
Ephesus, 3rd Ecumenical Council at (431): 8; condemnation of the heresy of Nestorius, 8, 10, 11; St. Cyril's defense of Christian doctrine, 9.
Ephesus, Robber Synod of. See Robber Synod of Ephesus.
Epistles, Dogmatic: of St. Agatho to 6th Ecum. Council, 24; of St. Leo I to 4th Ecum. Council, 15.
Eucharist, Sacrament of Holy, discussed at Council of Trent, 98.
Eugene IV, Pope: dissolves Council of Basel, 74 recalls decree of dissolution, 75 seeks union with Greek Church, 76 complains of presumption of the council, 77 dissolves Council of Basel, 77 attends Councils of Ferrara and Florence, 78 work for union with Eastern Church, 79, 80, 82.
Euphemia, St., church of, 15.
Eusebius, Bishop of Nicomedia, friend of Arius, 2.
Eusthatius, Bishop of Antioch, 3.
Eutyches: author of heresy of Monophysitism, 13; excommunicated by Synod of Constantinople, 13; appeals to St. Leo I, 13; condemned by 4th Ecum. Council, 16.
Eutychians, accusation against Council of Chalcedon, 19.
Extreme Unction, Sacrament of, discussed at Council of Trent, 99.

Faith, profession of, Council of Trent, 106.
Farnese, Cardinal, opens 18th Ecum. Council, 86.
Ferrara, Union Council of, 79.
Filioque, addition to Creed, 56.
Flavian, Patriarch of Constantinople, opposes Eutyches, 13.
Florence, third place of Union Council, 80.
Francis, St., of Assisi, at 12th Ecum. Council, 50.
Franciscans: controversy on obligation of vow of poverty, 63; Rule, approved by 15th Ecum. Council, 63; founders of Monti di pietà, 88.
Frederick II, excommunicated by 13th Ecum. Council, 54.

Germanus, Patriarch of Constantinople, opposes iconoclasm, 29.
Gonzaga, Hercules, legate to Council of Trent, 101.
Gratian, Emperor, 5.
Greek Union: discussed at 14th Ecum. Council, 57; at 17th Ecum. Council, 78, 82.
Gregory I, St., warning to Honorius I, 27.
Gregory, bishop of Neo-Caesarea, 31.
Gregory of Nazianzen, writings, 5.
Gregory VII, Pope, denounces investiture, 38.
Gregory X: opens 14th Ecum. Council, 56; brings about Greek Union, 57.
Gregory XI: lawful Pope, 65 sends plenipotentiary to Council of Constance, 69; abdicates, 69.
Gregory Asbestas, Bishop of Syracuse. See Asbestas, Gregory.

Hadrian I, St.: convokes 7th Ecum. Council, 30; confirms acts, 32.
Hadrian II, Pope, annuls decrees of pseudo-council of Constantinople, 34; sends legates to 8th Ecum. Council, 34.
Henry II, of England, murders Thomas á Becket, 44.
Henry II, of France, opponent of Council of Trent, 97.
Henry IV, and investiture, 38.
Henry V, and investiture, 38.
Heraclius, Emperor, issues *Ekthesis*, 24.
Hergenroether, Cardinal, *Anti-Janus,* 109.
Holy Eucharist, Sacrament of, discussed at Council of Trent, 98.

Holy Ghost: divinity of, 7; procession of, 56.
Holy Land: recovery and aid for Holy Land discussed at 12th Ecum. Council, 48; at, 4th Ecum. Council, 56; at 15th Ecum. Council, 63.
Holy Orders, Sacrament of, discussed at Council of Trent, 104.
Honorius I, Pope: and Monothelitism, 23 word on, 27.
Honorius III, decrees Crusade, 52.
Hosius, Bishop, at 1st Ecum. Council, 2, 4.
Huss, John, Bohemian heretic, 71.
Hussites: Crusade against, demands rejected by Council of Basel, 75.

Ibas, Bishop of Edessa, 16, 21.
Iconoclasm, 29.
Iconoclastic Synod of Constantinople, 30.
Ignatius, Patriarch of Constantinople, 33.
Indulgences, 105.
Infants, Communion of, 102.
Innsbruck, opposition assembly at, 103.
Innocent II, Pope, convokes 10th Ecum. Council, 42.
Innocent III, Pope, convokes 12th Ecum. Council, 48.
Innocent IV, Pope, convokes 13th Ecum. Council, 53.
Investiture: abolition of, at Lateran Council, 37; Henry IV and, 38. Henry V and, 38; Callistus II and, 38; Cardinals Lambert, Saxo and Gregory and, 41; installation "by sceptre," 39.
Irenaeus, Count, friend of Nestorius, 11.
Irene, Empress, petitions for 7th Ecum. Council, 30.

James of Nisibis, at 1st Ecum. Council, 3.
Janus, of Doellinger, summary of historical objections to papal infallibility, 109.
Jerome of Ascoli (Nicholas IV), Franciscan, and Greek Union, 55.
Jerome of Prague, heretic, condemned at 16th Ecum. Council, 72.
Joachim, Abbot, writings condemned by 12th Ecum. Council, 50.
John of Antioch: friend of Nestorius, 10 excommunicated by 3rd Ecum. Council, 13.
John IV, Pope, defends Pope Hononus I, 27.
John of Reggio, papal legate to 6th Ecum. Council, 24.

John Parastron, Franciscan sent by Gregory X to labor for Greek Union, 55.
John XXIII, anti-pope: convokes Council of Constance, 67; his position untenable, 67; flees, 68; deposed by council and arrested, 68; Martin V intervenes for him, 70.
Judicatum, decree of Pope Vigilius, 20.
Julius II, Pope: frustrates action of refractory cardinals, 85; convokes 18th Ecum. Council, 85; brings about abolition of Pragmatic Sanction, 87.
Julius III, Pope, at Council of Trent, 97.
Justification, decree on, published at Council of Trent, 95.
Justin I, Emperor, 19.
Justinian, Emperor, 19.
Juvenal of Jerusalem, deposed at 4th Ecum. Council, 15.

Kenrick, Peter R., Archbishop of St. Louis, opponent of papal infallibility, 111.
Knights Templars: trial and suppression at 5th Ecum. Council, 60; charges against, 61; arrest in France, 61; Clement V protests arrest, 61; bull *Vox in excelso* suppressing, 62; bull *Ad providam* disposing of, 63.

Laetare Jerusalem, bull of Paul III, opening Council of Trent, 93.
Laetentur caeli, dogmatic definition of Union Council of Florence, 81.
Lambert, Cardinal Bishop of Ostia, deals with Henry V on investiture, 38.
Lateran, 9th Ecumenical Council at (1123): purpose of, 37 means of investiture, 39; convoked by Callistus II, 39.

10th Ecumenical Council at purpose of council, 41 convoked by Innocent II, 42; papal schism removed, 42; heresy of Peter of Bruys condemned, 42.

11th Ecumenical Council at (1179): purpose of council, 44; convoked by Alexander III, 45; issues regulations to be observed in papal elections, 45; condemns Albigensian heresy, 46; canons issued, 46.

12th Ecumenical Council at (1215): purpose of council, 47 convoked by bull *Vineam Domini Sabaoth,* 48; orders contributions to Crusade, 49; decree on

INDEX 121

yearly confession and pascal Communion, 49; regulations regarding marriage, 49; issues definition of Faith, 50.

    18th Ecumenical Council at (1512–17): convoked by Julius II, 85; condemns pseudo-Council of Pisa, 86; abolishes Pragmatic Sanction of Bourges, 87; on death of Pope Julius II, council is continued by Leo X, 87; council endorses Franciscan *Monti di Pietà,* 88; regulations concerning printing of books, 89.

Lay Chalice: granted to Bohemia by Council of Constance, 75; regulations of Council of Trent, 102.

League of Lombardy, against invasion of Frederick Barbarossa, 44.

Leo I, St., Pope, *Dogmatic Epistle,* 15, 16; confirms 4th Ecum. Council, 18 rejects canon 15, 18.

Leo I, Emperor, 19.

Leo II, St., Pope, confirms Acts of 6th Ecum. Council, 27; corrects condemnation of Honorius I, 28.

Leo III, Emperor, originator of iconoclasm, 29.

Leo X, Pope, continues 18th Ecum. Council at Lateran, 87; sanctions Franciscan *Monti di Pieta,* 88; condemns prevalent errors, 88 regulations for printing of books, 89.

Lepers, canon of 11th Ecum. Council regarding, 46.

Lothaire, crowned Emperor by Innocent II, 41.

Lull, Blessed Raymond, Franciscan tertiary, 64.

Lyons, 13th Ecumenical Council at (1245): charges against Frederick II, 52; Innocent IV calls council, 53; Frederick defended to council, 53; Frederick excommunicated, 54; his subjects absolved allegiance, 54.

    14th Ecumenical Council at (1274): purposes of council, 55; Gregory X sends Franciscans to Constantinople, 55; ways and means to help Holy Land, 56; Greek envoys arrive at Lyons, 57; addition *Filioque* to Creed, 57 St. Bonaventure's work at council, 58; two important canons, 58.

Macarius, Bishop of Jerusalem, at 1st Ecum. Council, 3.

Macarius, Patriarch of Antioch, 25.

Macedonius, author of Macedonianism, 5.

Magnaura Palace, 32, 35.

Malatesta, Cardinal, plenipotentiary of Gregory XII, 69.

Marathonius, Bishop of Nicaea, 5.

Marcellus, of Ancyra, 3.

Marcian, Emperor: asks Leo I to convoke a general council, 15; edicts enforcing decrees of Council of Chalcedon, 18.

Maret, Dean of Sorbonne, and papal infallibility, 109.

Marianus, papal legate to 8th Ecum. Council, 35.

Maris, Bishop of Chalcedon, refuses to sign condemnation of Arius, 4.

Mark, Archbishop of Ephesus, opponent of Union Council of Florence, 80.

Maronites: at 17th Ecum. Council, 83; at 18th Ecum. Council, 89.

Marriages, clandestine, 49, 104.

Martin I, St., condemns Monothelitism, 24.

Martin V, Pope: elected at 16th Ecum. Council, 70; intervenes in behalf John XXIII, 71; asked by Sigismund to reside in Germany, 72; enters Rome in 1420, 72.

Mass, Sacrifice of, provisions of Council of Trent concerning, 103.

Massarelli, 97.

Maternity, Divine, of the Blessed Virgin Mary, 10.

Mathieu, Cardinal, and papal infallibility, 109.

Maximian, Archbishop of Constantinople, 12.

Maximus, Bishop of Constantinople, 6.

Medici, John Cardinal de (Pius IV) re-opens Council of Trent (3rd Period), 101; assisted by St. Charles Borromeo, 101; issues bull of confirmation, 106.

Meletians, aided by Arius, 2.

Meletius, abolition of schism of, 4.

Memnon, Archbishop of Ephesus, at 3rd Ecum. Council, 10.

Michael III, Emperor, separated Eastern Church from Rome, 33.

Michael Caerularius, Patriarch of Constantinople, 36.

Michael Palaeologus, Emperor, desires union with Rome, 55.

Mohammedans, 46.

Monophysitism: heresy of Eutyches, 13; *Dogmatic Epistle* of St. Leo I, 15; condemned at 4th Ecum. Council, 16.

Monothelitism: heresy of Sergius, 23; Emperor Heraclius issues *Ekthesis*, 24; Pope St. Agatho sends *Dogmatic Epistle* to 6th Ecum. Council, 24; Sergius and followers anathematized, 26; Pope St. Leo II confirms acts with correction, 27; and Pope Honorius, 27.

Montanus, heresy of, 1.

Monti di Pieta charity banks founded by Franciscans, 88; sanctioned by 18th Ecum. Council, 89.

Mopsuestia, Theodore of, writings condemned at 5th Ecum. Council, 21.

Morone, cardinal legate at Council of Trent, 104.

McQuaid, Bishop of Rochester, and papal infallibility, 111.

Naples, "Brothers of Three Points" hold council at, 110.

Navagero, cardinal legate at Council of Trent, 103.

Nazianzen, St. Gregory of, writings, 5.

Nectarius, Bishop of Constantinople, presides at 2nd Ecum. Council, 6.

Nestorians, at 57th Ecum. Council, 83.

Nestorius, Patriarch of Constantinople: his heresy, 8; writes to Pope St. Celestine, 9; excommunicated by Roman Synod, 9; anathemas of St. Cyril, 9; answers with counter-anathemas, 9; deposed and excommunicated by 3rd Ecum. Council, 10; banished, 12.

Nicaea, 1st Ecumenical Council at (325): purpose of council, 1; Arius and his heresy, 2; prelates attending, 2; profession of Faith, 3; condemnation of Arius and his heresy, 4; celebration of Easter, 4; abolition of the schism of Meletius, 4; council is honored, 4.

  7th Ecumenical Council at (787): 29; purpose of, condemnation of iconoclasm, 29, 31; Pope Hadrian sends legates to, 30; definition of Faith, 32; iconoclasm condemned by, 31.

Nicene-Constantinopolitan Creed, 7.

Nicephorus, Bishop of Nicaea, refuses to sign Roman definition, 35.

Nicholas I, Pope: asked to confirm election of Photius, 34; sends two legates to investigate heresy, 34; annuls election of Photius, 34; Pope is deposed by Photius, 34.

Olivi, Peter, Franciscan Spiritual, errors condemned, 63.

Oriental languages, study of, decreed by 15th Ecum. Council, 64.

Palaeologus, John, Greek Emperor, 78, 82.

Palaeologus, Michael, desires return to Rome, 55.

Papal infallibility: opponents of, 109, 111; debate at Vatican Council, 112; decree on, 113.

Paphnutius, of Thebais, at 1st Ecum. Council, 3.

Parastron, John, Franciscan, and Greek Union, 55.

Paschasinus, papal legate to 4th Ecum. Council, 15.

Paterno, Abundantius of, papal legate to 6th Ecum. Council, 24.

Pastor Aeternus, Dogmatic Constitution of Pius IX, 113.

Paul III: convokes Ecum. Council of Trent, 92; appoints legates, 92; presides first period of council, 92; suspends council in 1549, 96.

Paul IV, Pope, 100.

Pelagius I, recognizes 5th Ecum. Council, 21.

Penance, canonical, prescribed for repentant bishops by 8th Ecum. Council, 36.

Penance, Sacrament of, discussed at Council of Trent, 99.

Peter Chrysologus, St.; Eutyches' appeal to, 13.

Peter of Bruys, heretic, condemned by 10th Ecum. Council, 42.

Peter of Tarentaise, at 14th Ecum. Council, 56.

Peter Olivi, Franciscan Spiritual, errors condemned, 63.

Philip the Fair, King of France enemy of Boniface VIII, 60; and Knights Templars, 61, 62.

Photius, Patriarch of Constantinople: schismatic, 33; intrudes upon See of Constantinople, 33; deposes and excommunicates Pope Nicholas I, 34; cited before 8th Ecum. Council, 35; is

excommunicated, 35; his writings burned, 36.
Pius IX, Pope: inquires into advisability of holding ecumenical council, 108; letters to bishops of Latin and Oriental Rite, 108; issues bull *Aeterni Patris* convoking Vatican Council, 108; issues constitution *Dei Filius,* 112; issues constitution *Pastor aeternus,* 112; defines infallibility of Pope, 113; prorogues Vatican Council, 114.
Polychronius, monk, 26.
Pole, Reginald Cardinal, papal legate to Council of Trent, 92.
Pope, election of, discussed at 11th Ecum. Council, 45, 58.
Poverty, obligation of, in Franciscan Order, 63.
Pragmatic Sanction of Bourges, 87.
Prague, Jerome of, heretic burnt at stake, 72.
Procopius, leader of Hussites at Council of Basel, 75.
Protestants, and Council of Trent, 94, 100.
Pseudo-Councils: of Ephesus (Robber Synod), 14; of Constantinople, endorsing iconoclasm, 30; of Pisa, convoked by refractory Cardinals, 87.
Pulcheria. Empress, and 4th Ecum. Council, 14, 17.
Purgatory, doctrine of, 105.

Ravenna, Guibert of, anti-pope created by Henry IV, 38.
Reform of calendar, 89.
Relics, veneration of: 7th Ecum. Council, 32; Council of Trent, 105.
Religious orders, useless multiplication of, 59.
Robber Synod of Ephesus, condemned at 4th Ecum. Council, 14, 15.
Robert of Geneva, anti-pope Clement VII, 65.
Rodoald, Bishop of Porto, sent by Nicholas I to investigate case of Photius, 34.
Roemische Briefe, by Doellinger, 111.
Roger of Sicily, 41.

Sacraments, Decree regarding, passed at Council of Trent, 95.
Sanction, Pragmatic, of Bourges, abrogated by 18th Ecum. Council, 87.
Saxo, papal legate, deals with Henry V on investiture, 38.
Scriptures, Canonical, first decree of Council of Trent, 94.
Sergius, Patriarch of Constantinople: author of Monothelitism, 23; tries to ensnare Pope Honorius I, 23; condemned by 6th Ecum. Council, 26.
Sigismund: strives to put an end to Western Schism, 67; convokes the Council of Constance, 67; supervises deposition of anti-pope John XXIII, 68; goes to Benedict XIII to obtain his resignation, 70.
Sylvester, St. I, Pope, 1st Ecum. Council at Nicaea, 3, 4.
Simony, prevalent in 12th century, 37.
Sophia, St., church of, 8th Ecum. Council held, 35.
Sophronius, St., Patriarch of Jerusalem, 23.
Spalding, Archbishop of Baltimore, supporter of papal infallibility, 114.
Sturmius, St., of Fulda, 43.

Tarasius, Patriarch of Constantinople, opponent of iconoclasm, 30.
Templars, Knights, suppressed at 15th Ecum. Council, 62.
Thaddeus of Suessia, Chancellor of Frederick II, 53.
Thaleia, work of Arius, 2.
Theobald, Archbishop of Canterbury, attends 10th Ecum. Council, 43.
Theodosius, Bishop of Ephesus, defends iconoclasm, 29.
Theodosius, Bishop of Amorium, abjures iconoclasm, 31.
Theodosius I, convokes 2nd Ecum. Council, 5, 7.
Theodosius II, confirms Acts of Robber Synod of Ephesus, 14.
Theodore of Mopsuestia, writings condemned by 5th Ecum. Council, 21.
Theodoret of Cyrus, writings condemned by 5th Ecum. Council, 21.
Theophilus, bishop of Photian faction, 35.
Theonas of Mamarica, refuses to condemn Arius, 4.
Theotokos (Mother of God), doctrine at 3rd Ecum. Council, 10.
Third Person of the Blessed Trinity, divinity of, 6.
Thomas, St., Aquinas, called to 4th Ecum. Council, 56.
Thomas, bishop of Claudiopolis, defends

iconoclasm, 29.
Three Chapters, condemned at 5th Ecum. Council, 21.
Transubstantiation, discussed at 12th Ecum. Council, 50; at Council of Trent, 97.
Trent, 19th Ecum. Council at (1545–1563): purposes of, 91; council convoked by bull *Laetare Jerusalem* of Paul III, 93; right to vote at, 93; title of council, 93; attitude of Protestants toward, 94; Canonical Scriptures, first decree, 94; doctrine of Immaculate Conception, 95; justification, 95; Sacraments discussed, 95; transferred to Bologna, 96; second period of, 97; Penance and Extreme Unction discussed, 99; council suspended by Julius III, 100; third period of, 102; decree on Holy Eucharist, 102; Sacrifice of Mass discussed, 103; Holy Orders discussed, 104; Matrimony discussed, 104; Purgatory, veneration of saints and relics, indulgences, 105; confirmation of acts by Pius IV, 106; how received by the various powers, 106; Profession of Faith, 106; Catechism of Council of Trent, 106.
Treuga Dei (Truce of God), 46.
Typus, edict of Constans II, in favor of Monothelitism, 24.

Union, Greek; at 14th Ecum. Council at Lyons, 55; at Union Council at Florence, 17th Ecum. Council, 80.
Urban VI, Pope, 65.

Vatican, 20th Ecum. Council at (1869–1870): purpose of, condemnation of prevalent errors, and definition of papal infallibility, 108 convoked by bull *Aeterni Patris,* 108; invitations to Eastern bishops and Protestants, 108; convocation rouses enmity, 109; appointment of four committees, 109; opening of council, 110; constitution *Dei Filius,* 112; debate on papal infallibility, 112; constitution *Pastor aeternus,* 113; definition of papal infallibility, 113; bishops voting against definition, 113; council prorogued, 114.
Veneration of saints and relics discussed at 7th Ecum. Council, 31; at Council of Trent, 105.
Victor IV, anti-pope, 41.
Vienne, 15th Ecumenical Council at (1311–1312): 60; to examine case of Knights Templars, 61; council convoked by bull *Alma Mater,* 61; two commissions examine case of Knights Templars, 62; Clement V issues bull suppressing Knights Templars, 62; bull *Ad providam,* 63; bull *Exivi de paradiso,* 63; help for the Holy Land, 63.
Vigilius, Pope: goes to Constantinople, 19; issues *Judicatum,* 21; issues *Constitutum,* 21; issues second *Constitutum,* 21; is banished, 21; condemns Three Chapters, 21.
Vincentius, papal legate to 1st Ecum. Council, 3.
Vineam Domini, bull of Innocent III, convoking 12th Ecum. Council, 48.
Vitus, papal legate to 1st Ecum. Council, 3.
Voltaire, eulogy of Alexander III, 44.
Vox in excelso, bull of Clement V, suppressing Knights Templars, 62.
Vulgate, authentic edition of Holy Scriptures, 4th Session of Council of Trent, 94.

Waldenses, heretics condemned at 12th Ecum. Council, 49.
Western Schism, 65.
Worms, Concordat of, abolition of investiture, 39.
Wyclif, heresies of: condemned at synod in London, 71; at Council of Constance, 71.

Zachary, bishop of Anagni, investigates case of Photius, 34.
Zachary, bishop of Photian faction, 35.
Zeno, Emperor, 19.